HOUR OF THE DAWN

The Life of the Báb

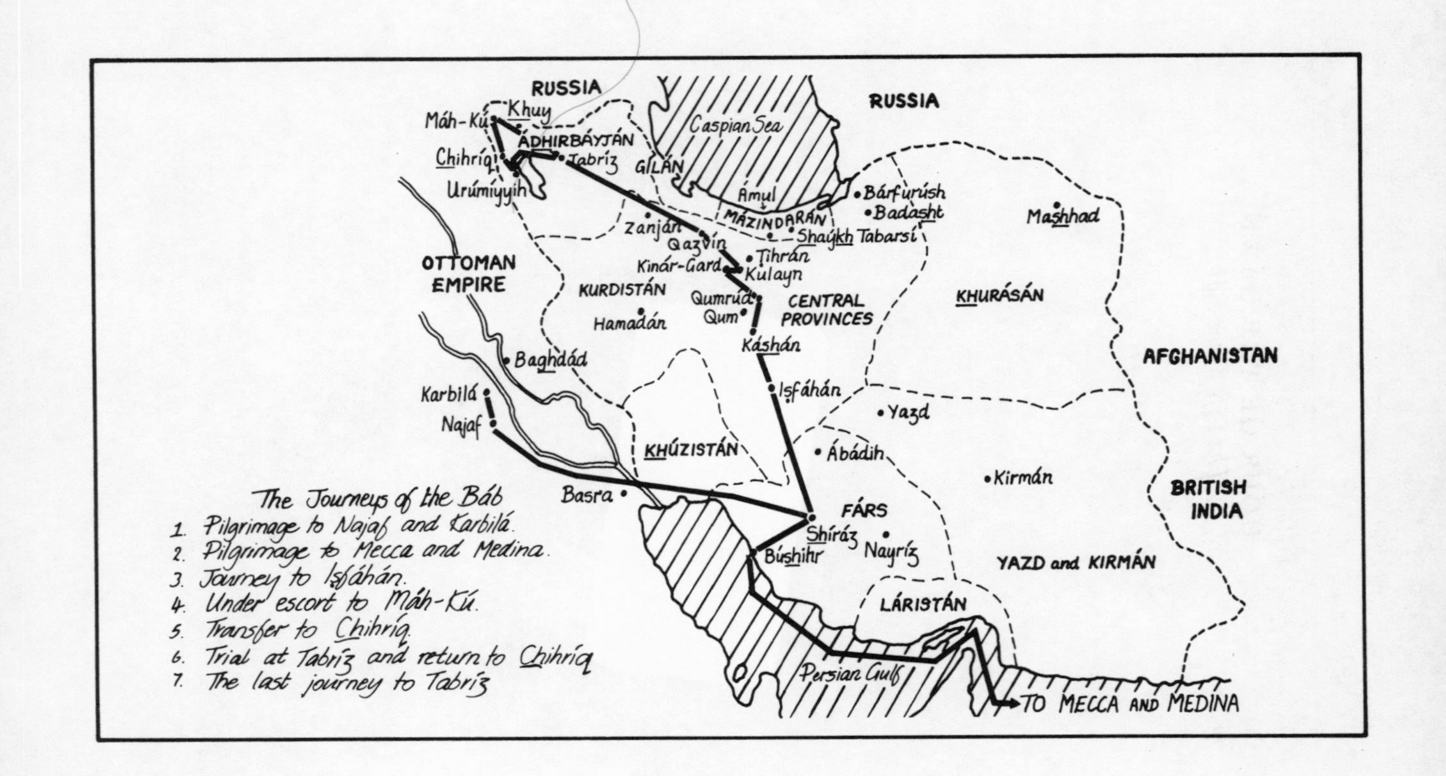
RUSSIA
Máh-Kú
Khuy
ÁDHIRBÁYJÁN
Chihríq
Tabríz
Urúmiyyih
Caspian Sea
GÍLÁN
Ámul
MÁZINDARÁN
Bárfurúsh
Badasht
Shaykh Tabarsí
Mashhad
Zanján
Qazvín
Tihrán
Kinár-Gard
Kulayn
OTTOMAN EMPIRE
KURDISTÁN
Qumrúd
Qum
CENTRAL PROVINCES
KHURÁSÁN
Hamadán
Káshán
AFGHANISTAN
Baghdád
Karbilá
Najaf
Iṣfáhán
Yazd
KHÚZISTÁN
Ábádih
Kirmán
BRITISH INDIA
Basra
FÁRS
Shíráz
Nayríz
Búshihr
YAZD and KIRMÁN
LÁRISTÁN
Persian Gulf
TO MECCA AND MEDINA
The Journeys of the Báb
1. Pilgrimage to Najaf and Karbilá.
2. Pilgrimage to Mecca and Medina.
3. Journey to Iṣfáhán.
4. Under escort to Máh-Kú.
5. Transfer to Chihríq.
6. Trial at Tabríz and return to Chihríq
7. The last journey to Tabríz

HOUR OF THE DAWN

The Life of the Báb

based on the works of
Nabíl-i-A'ẓam and H. M. Balyuzi

by

Mary Perkins

GEORGE RONALD
OXFORD

GEORGE RONALD, Publisher
46 High Street, Kidlington, Oxford OX5 2DN

Reprinted 2001

*A calogue record for this book is available
from the British Library*

ISBN 0–85398–252–X

Phototypset by Sunrise Setting, Torquay, Devon
Printed and bound in Great Britain
by Cromwell Press Ltd, Trowbridge

CONTENTS

	PROLOGUE	1
I	WITNESSES OF THE DAWN 1819–1844	13
	1 Birth and childhood	15
	2 Youth and marriage	19
	3 'O well-beloved'	26
	4 Mullá Ḥusayn reaches Shíráz	28
	5 The Báb declares His mission	30
II	RAISING THE CALL OF A NEW DAY 1844	39
	6 The Letters of the Living	41
	7 'Arise in His Name'	45
	8 The first to suffer	48
	9 Mullá Ḥusayn undertakes a special mission to Ṭihrán	51
III	PILGRIMAGE AND SEIZURE September 1844 – July 1845	57
	10 'I am that Qá'im'	59
	11 A tumult in Shíráz	64
	12 The Báb is arrested	69
IV	SHÍRÁZ July 1845 – September 1846	73
	13 The Báb speaks from the pulpit	75
	14 Persia in distress	81
	15 The Sháh's envoy	85
	16 Farewell to Shíráz	91

V IṢFÁHÁN October 1846 – March 1847 97

17 The Báb is made welcome in Iṣfáhán 99
18 The Grand Vizier stirs up trouble 103
19 Manúchihr Khán shelters the Báb 107

VI KÁSHÁN TO TABRÍZ March 1847 – July 1847 111

20 A secret summons to Ṭihrán 113
21 The Grand Vizier plays for time 117
22 The road to Tabríz 120
23 Into custody 124

VII MÁH-KÚ July 1847 – April 1848 127

24 A strict confinement 129
25 The prison doors open 132
26 The Báb sets down His teachings 135
27 Mullá Ḥusayn visits Máh-Kú 139

VIII CHIHRÍQ April 1848 – September 1848 145

28 Another strict confinement fails 147
29 The Letters of the Living and the Conference of Badasht 150
30 Trial at Tabríz 158

IX AN OCEAN OF SORROW September 1848 – June 1850 165

31 The siege of Shaykh Ṭabarsí 167
32 The Seven Martyrs of Ṭihrán 174
33 Nayríz and Zanján 178

X TABRÍZ July 1850 183

34 Anís, the Báb's chosen companion 185
35 Dark noon 189

EPILOGUE 195

A Note on Sources 199
List of Names 203
Some Persian and Arabic Terms 210
A Few Dates 212

ILLUSTRATIONS

Frontispiece	Map of Persia, showing the journeys of the Báb
Prologue	The Shrine of the Imám Ḥusayn at Karbilá
I	Shíráz, from the Alláh-u-Akbar pass
II	The room in the House of the Báb in Shíráz in which He declared His Mission
III	The Ka'bih at Mecca
IV	The pulpit in Shíráz from which the Báb addressed the congregation
V	The Maydán-i-Sháh in Iṣfáhán
VI	The camp of Kulayn
VII	The fortress of Máh-Kú
VIII	The mountain and fortress of Chihríq
IX	Site of martyrdoms at Nayríz
X	Part of the citadel wall at Tabríz
Epilogue	The Shrine of the Báb

This book is dedicated to the shining memory of
Nabíl-i-A'ẓam and Ḥasan M. Balyuzi
with love and gratitude

'No eye hath beheld so great an
outpouring of bounty, nor hath
any ear heard of such a revelation
of lovingkindness.'

Bahá'u'lláh

PROLOGUE

This is the story of the Báb, the herald of Bahá'u'lláh. The Báb and Bahá'u'lláh are the latest of God's Messengers to the world; their message is for every person alive today.

The coming of a Messenger of God is so rare and great an event in human history that we know only the names of a few who have lived on our earth. Krishna, Abraham, Moses, Zoroaster, Buddha, Jesus and Muḥammad were Messengers of God: there were others before them in other parts of the world whose names we do not now know. Wherever there have been people, God has sent a Messenger to them with teachings that they need and can understand.

God has always left us free to choose whether or not we follow His Messengers and they have always suffered at our hands. Armed only with the weapons of love, compassion and the power of the Word of God which they reveal, each one of them has changed the hearts of a handful of people, and each one has brought spiritual teachings that have changed the world. Led by their guidance, we have stumbled upwards and onwards, step by halting step, towards that Day each one of them has foretold, the Day when all humankind shall live as one family, when there shall be peace and justice throughout the earth.

Each Messenger who has come to the earth has given guidance in His Writings and teachings about another Messenger who will come after Him, usually after a period of many centuries. All the world's great religions look forward to a time of justice and peace on earth.

In the late eighteenth and early nineteenth centuries, some believers within both Christianity and Islám anticipated eagerly the coming of a world teacher who would bring peace to all the world's peoples. In the 1780s a Persian Muslim named Shaykh Aḥmad began to teach that the time had come when the Promised One, the Messenger of God awaited by the entire Islamic world, would soon appear on earth.

Shaykh Aḥmad's family came from Arabia, but he spent the first forty years of his life on one of the small islands of Bahrain, in the gulf that divides the Arabian peninsula and Persia. Shaykh Aḥmad was a man of saintly character and a devout Muslim. He was deeply troubled by the corruption and strife which he witnessed amongst his fellow Muslims and by the ignorance and fanaticism displayed by the various contending sects of Islám. He prayed and worked for the removal of these abuses but he came gradually to understand that no programme of reform, however radical and thorough, could ever succeed in restoring the early strength and purity of Islám.

He further realised that only the power and authority of a new Messenger of God could clear away the mists of prejudice and ignorance in which the followers of Muḥammad were shrouded. He also became convinced that he was living at a time spoken of by Muḥammad, when God would again send a Messenger to the world to refresh and revive the hearts of men. He began to understand that his own life's work lay in preparing the hearts of people for this long-awaited Messenger. Shaykh Aḥmad's inner conviction that such a tremendous event was shortly to occur made it impossible for him to remain on his island home. He felt that he must leave all that was dear and familiar to him and travel far and wide to spread the good news that lit his heart.

When this momentous realisation dawned upon Shaykh Aḥmad, he was already forty years old and was fully aware of the perils and dangers of such an enterprise, but he bade farewell to his family and friends, left all that he possessed, put his trust firmly in God and set out on the first stage of his journey. He went northwards from his island home to Basra at the head of the gulf waters. From Basra he travelled, either on foot or on a camel, west and then north across the desert, along the valley of the Euphrates in the company of other devout Muslims bound for the holy cities of Najaf and Karbilá.

In order to understand the significance of these two cities, Najaf and Karbilá, it is necessary to know a little of the history of Islám. Islám is divided into two main sects, the Shí'ihs and the Sunnís. This division occurred soon after the death of Muḥammad and continues to the present day. Some of the followers of Muḥammad (Shí'ih Muslims) believe that Muḥammad appointed a successor from His own family. Other followers of Muḥammad (Sunní Muslims) believe that no successor was appointed by Muḥammad but that the successor to the Prophet should be elected by the believers.

Both these great branches of the faith of Islám await the coming of a Messenger of God. The Shí'ihs await the coming of the Qá'im (He Who ariseth) while the Sunnís await the coming of the Mihdí (One Who is guided). At the time when Shaykh Aḥmad lived, this belief in the coming of the Qá'im was so strong an element in the faith of some Shí'ite Muslims and His appearance was looked forward to with such excitement and awe that whenever the word 'Qá'im' was spoken, they would rise to their feet and stand in reverent silence. Shaykh Aḥmad was a Shí'ih Muslim but he was determined to direct his call to all the followers of Muḥammad, Sunnís and Shí'ihs alike.

For a thousand years, devout Shí'ite Muslims have travelled on pilgrimage to the two holy cities of Najaf and Karbilá, oases of beauty, sanctity and learning in the surrounding sea of the desert. Najaf is revered as the resting-place of the Imám 'Alí, the cousin, son-in-law and first disciple of Muḥammad. S͟hí'ih Muslims believe that Muḥammad himself appointed 'Alí as His own direct successor. Karbilá is revered as the resting-place of the Imám Ḥusayn, the young grandson of Muḥammad, who was martyred on the nearby plain of Karbilá in AD 680. Abbas, the brother of Ḥusayn, is also buried at Karbilá. It is a tenet of S͟hí'ite belief that once the Qá'im has appeared, the Imám Ḥusayn will reappear together with the seventy-two companions who were killed with him at Karbilá.

S͟hayk͟h Aḥmad visited both Najaf and Karbilá to pray at the shrines and then settled in Karbilá. He began systematically to study and unravel the meaning of the Islamic verses and traditions which foreshadow the coming of a new Messenger of God. Many people were attracted by his saintly character and by his great learning and came to hear him teach. He was recognised by the other learned Muslim teachers as an authority on the Islamic writings and was declared to hold the rank of mujtahid.

S͟hayk͟h Aḥmad soon stood out amongst the other mujtahids in the city both on account of his learning and his fearlessness, but he cared nothing for fame and despised the honours that were heaped upon him. He might have stayed in Karbilá for many years but a great yearning arose in his heart to travel to Persia, for he felt that, in that land, God would reveal to him more of the mystery of the coming Messenger. He told no one of this but informed his students that he was going on pilgrimage to the holy city of Mas͟hhad. It is the desire of most S͟hí'ite Muslims to visit Mas͟hhad at least once in their lives in order to pray at the shrine of the eighth Imám, the Imám Riḍá.

S͟hayk͟h Aḥmad chose the difficult sea route to Persia rather than the easier overland route and went by way of Bús͟hihr, a busy port on the humid and barren Persian coast. He stayed only a few days in Bús͟hihr and then, following the promptings of his heart, went north-east through the dry hills of Fárs province, a journey of about one hundred miles.

Shíráz has had a turbulent history over the last thousand years of earthquake, flood, famine and plague but it has been famous for many centuries for the words of its poets, for its exquisite silk carpets and for the beauty of its rose gardens. When Shaykh Aḥmad first looked down on Shíráz, the old city was still packed in tightly behind a strong defensive wall above which the tops of pine and cypress promised shade and the domes of the city's mosques gleamed, offering spiritual refreshment, peace and beauty in a dry land. Just inside the city wall there bloomed an encircling belt of greenery and flowers enticing weary travellers with the scents of saffron and jasmine, roses and sweet herbs. Shaykh Aḥmad knew that in future centuries the fame of Shíráz as the birthplace of a Messenger of God would eclipse all its past splendours.

Once inside the city, Shaykh Aḥmad felt himself drawn closer to the meaning of the mystery that filled his heart with awe and wonder. He lavished his praises on the city. The learned men of Shíráz, awed by the reputation of Shaykh Aḥmad, struggled to grasp the significance of his words but failed to understand their meaning.

'Wonder not,' Shaykh Aḥmad told them, 'for ere long the secret of my words will be made manifest to you. Among you there shall be a number who will live to behold the glory of a Day which the prophets of old have yearned to witness.'

Having awakened one or two receptive souls in Shíráz, Shaykh Aḥmad crossed the Zagros mountains to Yazd, a city on the edge of the great central desert of Persia. The climate of Yazd is harsh and its people tough, hard-working and suspicious of new ideas. In Yazd, Shaykh Aḥmad prayed and taught and wrote a number of books. While he was there a young man named Siyyid Káẓim came in search of him.

Siyyid Káẓim had heard of the famous teacher Shaykh

Aḥmad while living in his home-town of Rasht, near the Caspian Sea. He was twenty-two years old, an outstanding scholar but devoid of pride in his own learning. He was humble and gentle and devoted to God. The title 'Siyyid' means that he was descended from the family of the Prophet Muḥammad. As soon as he heard of Shaykh Aḥmad's teachings, he set out to find him. He reached Yazd in 1815 or 1816.

When Shaykh Aḥmad met Siyyid Káẓim, he realised at once that this was someone with whom he could share all that he had kept in his heart. He greeted Siyyid Káẓim joyfully.

'I welcome you, O my friend!' he said. 'How long and how eagerly have I waited for you to come and deliver me from the arrogance of this perverse people! . . .'

Siyyid Káẓim too was overjoyed for at last he had found someone who could satisfy his thirst for knowledge and understanding. He soon became the best student that Shaykh Aḥmad had ever had. Shaykh Aḥmad was able to entrust his group of students to the care of Siyyid Káẓim and set out on his pilgrimage to Mashhad.

Shaykh Aḥmad spent many hours in prayer and meditation at the holy shrine in Mashhad. He also spoke with the pilgrims who visited the shrine and was able to resolve many of the problems which agitated their hearts. He continued with undiminished zeal his work of preparing the hearts of the people for the coming of a new Messenger of God. While in Mashhad he was moved by a new sense of urgency as he felt that the time when this momentous event would take place was fast approaching. From Mashhad he summoned Siyyid Káẓim to meet with him and travel with him to Ṭihrán. In Ṭihrán, the capital of Persia, Shaykh Aḥmad was received by Fatḥ-'Alí Sháh, who declared that Shaykh Aḥmad was 'the glory of his nation and an ornament to his people'.

From Ṭihrán, Shaykh Aḥmad and Siyyid Káẓim travelled

to Kirmánsháh at the invitation of the Crown Prince of Persia, Muḥammad-'Alí Mírzá. There, Shaykh Aḥmad became aware that he had not many years left to him and thus felt even more strongly the urgency of his own mission. He selected a number of the most receptive of his students and strove earnestly to enlighten their hearts and to prepare them for the time of testing, trial and renewal that lay ahead. As before, Shaykh Aḥmad continued to single out Siyyid Káẓim and actively prepared him so that he would be able to carry on the work after his own passing.

When the year 1819 began, Shaykh Aḥmad and Siyyid Káẓim were still guests of the Crown Prince at Kirmánsháh. In that year, the first of the two awaited Messengers of God, 'Alí-Muḥammad, the Báb, was born in Shíráz. In the same year, 1819, Shaykh Aḥmad's own son, who was called Shaykh 'Alí, died. Shaykh Aḥmad himself comforted those who came to mourn his loss with these words:

'Grieve not, O my friends, for I have offered up my son, my own 'Alí, as a sacrifice for the 'Alí whose advent we all await. To this end have I reared and prepared him.'

At this time, the Crown Prince too died, quite suddenly, while still a young man, and after his death, Shaykh Aḥmad and Siyyid Káẓim took the road home to Karbilá.

On their arrival in the city, many of the most learned and famous men of Karbilá and Najaf thronged to see Shaykh Aḥmad. His reputation grew so great that some began to envy him. They spread lies and slander about him through the city and worked to undermine his reputation and authority. Shaykh Aḥmad, aware of his own approaching death, shared with Siyyid Káẓim all the knowledge that he had and urged him, after his own passing, to swiftly kindle every receptive heart.

Shaykh Aḥmad began to plan his own last journey of pilgrimage, for he longed to end his days near the shrine of

Muḥammad at Medina in Arabia. Siyyid Káẓim begged to be allowed to travel with him, at least as far as Najaf, but Shaykh Aḥmad refused to grant this request.

'You have no time to lose,' he said. 'Every fleeting hour should be fully and wisely utilised. You should gird up the loin of endeavour and strive day and night to rend asunder, by the grace of God and by the hand of wisdom and loving-kindness, those veils of heedlessness that have blinded the eyes of men. For verily I say, the Hour is drawing nigh, the Hour I have besought God to spare me from witnessing, for the earthquake of the Last Hour will be tremendous. You should pray to God to be spared the overpowering trials of that Day, for neither of us is capable of withstanding its sweeping force. Others, of greater endurance and power, have been destined to bear this stupendous weight, men whose hearts are sanctified from all earthly things, and whose strength is reinforced by the potency of His power.'

Shaykh Aḥmad appointed Siyyid Káẓim as his own chosen successor and instructed all his disciples to turn to him in his absence and after his own passing. He then said a fond farewell to the disciple whom he loved so dearly, encouraged him to be brave through all the trials that lay ahead and committed him to the care of God.

Siyyid Káẓim at once took up the challenge of working alone in Karbilá and taught with vigour and enthusiasm. As soon as Shaykh Aḥmad's opponents saw that he had left Karbilá and that he had left Siyyid Káẓim to teach on his own, they began a fierce attack. Siyyid Káẓim persevered with his work through all difficulties and wrote to Shaykh Aḥmad recounting all that was happening in Karbilá. He asked how long he must endure such trials and begged to be told when the Promised One would appear.

Shaykh Aḥmad received this letter while he was on his journey and wrote a kind reply.

'Be assured of the grace of your God,' he wrote. 'Be not grieved at their doings. The mystery of this Cause must needs be made manifest, and the secret of this Message must needs be divulged. I can say no more, I can appoint no time . . .'

Shaykh Aḥmad continued on his pilgrimage, confident that the message entrusted to him by God would be in safe keeping. He died in Mecca in 1826 and was buried near the tomb of Muḥammad. To the end of his long life, his radiant face mirrored forth the joy that lit his heart.

'Ere long', was his joyful promise, 'will the earth be turned into a paradise.'

When the news of Shaykh Aḥmad's passing reached Karbilá, his opponents renewed their attacks on Siyyid Káẓim, mocking his teachings, cursing him and even molesting him in the streets. Siyyid Káẓim continued his lonely mission steadfastly for another fifteen years. Then, in the 1840s, when he felt his situation was growing desperate, he sent a brilliant young student named Mullá Ḥusayn on a hazardous mission to Persia to gain the support of several of the leading Muslim teachers.

Mullá Ḥusayn was very young and so frail physically that his hand shook when he wrote, but he was eager of heart and steadfast of soul, and longed with his whole being for the coming of the Promised One. He instantly obeyed Siyyid Káẓim's request and left to travel alone to Persia. He was away from Karbilá for many months. While Mullá Ḥusayn was away, Siyyid Káẓim's problems in Karbilá increased dramatically as a rebellion broke out in the city.

Karbilá had been for many centuries a Shí'ite stronghold under the rule of the Sunní Ottoman rulers. Both Karbilá and Najaf had long been centres of revolt and intrigue against Ottoman rule. When the rebels in Karbilá, incited by the Shí'ite clergy, expelled the Ottoman governor, the central government in Constantinople at once sent an army, under the command of a new governor, to subdue the city. Siyyid Káẓim took a leading role in attempting to avert a siege but, despite his best efforts, he did not succeed in persuading the rebels to submit to the new governor.

In January 1843, after a siege of twenty-four days, the Ottoman army entered Karbilá and the soldiers killed thousands of its citizens. Only the house of Siyyid Káẓim was declared by the governor to be a sanctuary, but even there many died of suffocation as throngs of desperate men, women and children struggled to enter the already overcrowded rooms. When the dreadful siege was over, Siyyid Káẓim was exhausted. He was only fifty years old but he had worn himself out in his efforts to bring peace to Karbilá.

He redoubled his efforts to guide his followers in the time still left to him. He felt that the Promised One, who would inaugurate a new age of peace for all men, was already living on the earth and he appointed no successor to continue his work. Instead he urged his disciples, after his own death, to scatter and search for the One whose coming they awaited. He gave them some important guidance as to how they might recognise Him. He told them:

'He is of noble lineage. He is a descendant of the Prophet of God, of the family of Há<u>sh</u>im. He is young in age, and is possessed of innate knowledge. His learning is derived, not from the teachings of <u>Sh</u>ay<u>kh</u> Aḥmad, but from God. My knowledge is but a drop compared with the immensity of His knowledge; my attainments a speck of dust in the face of the wonders of His grace and power. Nay, immeasurable is the difference. He is of medium height, abstains from smoking and is of extreme devoutness and piety.'

Whenever he met with his disciples, Siyyid Káẓim urged them to make strenuous efforts and to be persevering in their quest.

'O my beloved companions!' he said to them all. 'Beware, beware, lest after me the world's fleeting vanities beguile you. Beware lest you wax haughty and forgetful of God. It is incumbent upon you to renounce all comfort, all earthly possessions and kindred, in your quest of Him who is the Desire of your hearts and of mine. Scatter far and wide, detach yourselves from all earthly things, and humbly and prayerfully beseech your Lord to sustain and guide you. Never relax in your determination to seek and find Him who is concealed behind the veils of glory.'

Soon after the siege of Karbilá, Siyyid Káẓim died peacefully but his passing caused a great tumult in the city as many mourned their loss. Mullá Ḥusayn was still away in Persia at the time. Unaware of the turn events had taken, he had accomplished all that Siyyid Káẓim had asked of him and sped back towards Karbilá with a joyous heart only to learn, on reaching the city, that his beloved teacher had died. He was deeply grieved but made every effort to cheer and strengthen his companions, for he found them all downcast. He called together a group of Siyyid Káẓim's most trusted and respected disciples and asked them what the last instructions of their master had been.

They told him that Siyyid Káẓim had again and again urged them to leave their homes and to scatter far and wide in their search for the Promised One.

'Why, then,' asked Mullá Ḥusayn, 'have you chosen to tarry in Karbilá?'

When they did not reply, Mullá Ḥusayn explained and repeated the instructions of Siyyid Káẓim and begged them to begin their search, but each one made some excuse. 'Our enemies are many and powerful,' said one. 'We must remain in this city and guard the vacant seat of our departed chief,' said others. 'It is incumbent upon me to stay and care for the children whom the Siyyid has left behind,' said another.

Mullá Ḥusayn saw that they were blind and foolish and realised that he could do nothing for them if they did not themselves want to search.

He left the other disciples of Siyyid Káẓim alone and went with only his brother and his young nephew to a quiet place where he could prepare himself for the coming search. He prayed, fasted and begged God to guide him. He meditated on all that Siyyid Káẓim had taught him and tried to strip himself of all selfishness so that he would be worthy to undertake the search.

While Mullá Ḥusayn was preparing himself in this way, a group of his fellow students, inspired by his example, joined him and also began to pray and fast. This group was led by a man called Mullá 'Alí. Mullá 'Alí was one of the foremost disciples of Siyyid Káẓim. He was very familiar with the teachings of Shaykh Aḥmad and was renowned for his vast learning. Mullá 'Alí wanted to ask Mullá Ḥusayn where he planned to start his search but every time that he approached him, he found him so deeply absorbed in prayer that he dared not disturb him.

After spending forty days in prayer and fasting, Mullá Ḥusayn, together with his two young companions, set out in the cool of the night. The golden dome of the Imám Ḥusayn glimmered in the moonlight and the city slept around them as they took the first steps in their momentous journey in search of the Promised One.

I

Witnesses of the Dawn

1819–1844

CHAPTER 1
BIRTH AND CHILDHOOD

On the 20th of October 1819 in the warm southern city of Shíráz, which Shaykh Aḥmad had visited and praised so highly, a child was born into a family of well-respected merchants. His father and mother, who were loved and respected by their fellow citizens, were both descendants of the Prophet Muḥammad. They named their son 'Alí-Muḥammad: He is known to the world as the Báb. The Báb means 'The Gate' and it is the title that 'Alí-Muḥammad took when he declared His mission, but that story comes later. Around the time that the Báb was born in Shíráz, Shaykh Aḥmad and Siyyid Káẓim reached Karbilá together from Kirmánsháh and settled there. Neither of them ever visited Persia again.

Even as a very young child the Báb was unlike other children. Those who visited His parents' home were struck by the purity and sweetness of His character, by His serenity and His extreme courtesy. He cared little for the pastimes of other children and chanted His prayers in a melodious, enraptured voice. He was handsome and dignified and his extraordinary knowledge and wisdom astounded all who met Him, yet He was humble and gentle and tender-hearted. He was in every way a remarkable child.

When the Báb was still a small child, His father died and His mother's brother, whose name was Ḥájí Mírzá Siyyid 'Alí, took care of Him and brought Him up as his own son.

When He was five years old, the Báb was sent to a school run by a teacher called Shaykh 'Ábid. Shaykh 'Ábid was a member of the Shaykhí sect, that is, he was a follower of Shaykh Aḥmad and Siyyid Káẓim. When the Báb arrived at his school, Shaykh 'Ábid was immediately struck by the beauty of character of his new pupil and by the remarkable knowledge that He showed.

One day, Shaykh 'Ábid asked the Báb to recite the opening words of the Qur'án. The Báb hesitated and pleaded that unless He were told the meaning of the words, He would not recite them. The pupils in Shaykh 'Ábid's school were taught to recite the Qur'án but they did not learn Arabic, the language in which the Qur'án is written, so they could not possibly understand the meaning of the Holy Book. On this occasion, Shaykh 'Ábid pretended that he could not explain the meaning of the words.

'I know what these words signify,' the Báb said politely. 'By your leave, I will explain them.'

Shaykh 'Ábid was so much astonished by the explanation that the Báb gave, by the beauty and power of His words, that he took the Báb home to His uncle. He said to Ḥájí Mírzá Siyyid 'Alí:

'I have brought Him back to you and commit Him to your vigilant protection . . . for He, verily, stands in no need of teachers such as I.'

Ḥájí Mírzá Siyyid 'Alí spoke sternly to his nephew.

'Have you forgotten my instructions?' he asked. 'Have I not already admonished You to follow the example of Your fellow pupils, to observe silence and to listen attentively to every word spoken by Your teacher?'

The Báb promised to obey His uncle's instructions and He returned to school where He showed, day after day, in the most courteous and humble manner, that He was possessed of an extraordinary wisdom and knowledge gained not from books nor from any human teacher but from God.

The school which the Báb attended was a small elementary

school and Shaykh 'Ábid was the only teacher. The boys received only the most basic education, learning to read and write, learning some basic arithmetic and practising handwriting exercises. They also read some Persian poetry and they were taught how to recite the Qur'án.

In addition to teaching boys, Shaykh 'Ábid had a small class for theological students. One day he held a long discussion with these students but he could not give them an answer to the problem they raised. He told them that he would consult some other books that evening and would give them an answer the next morning. The Báb happened to be listening to the discussion and when it was over, He began to speak. With sound reasoning He gave the answer that His teacher and the students sought. They were all amazed.

One day, the Báb came late to school. When Shaykh 'Ábid asked Him why He had come late, He said that He had been in the house of his 'Grandfather'. It is thus that the siyyids, the descendants of Muḥammad, refer to their revered ancestor, the Prophet Muḥammad. Shaykh 'Ábid told the Báb that He was only a child and that He need not spend so much of His time in prayer. The Báb replied quietly:

'I wish to be like My Grandfather.'

On Fridays, the Muslim day of rest, the teacher took his students to a garden where they could enjoy fresh air and beautiful scenery. On such days, the Báb would find a shady corner a little apart from the rest of the students where He would pray and meditate. The Báb did not often join in the games played by the other children but He was always kind and considerate. All of the members of His family, children and adults alike, paid great respect to their young relative.

Next door to the house of Ḥájí Mírzá Siyyid 'Alí, where the Báb spent his childhood, was the home of another relative, a great-uncle on His mother's side who was called Mírzá 'Alí. This great-uncle had a young daughter named

Khadíjih-Bagum. The Báb and Khadíjih-Bagum were much the same age and they knew each other as relatives, neighbours and playmates from their earliest years. Their lives were soon to be much more closely linked.

CHAPTER 2

YOUTH AND MARRIAGE

Apart from the great sorrow of losing His father, the Báb's childhood was a tranquil one. The Báb studied at Shaykh 'Ábid's school for six or seven years and left when He was thirteen. At fifteen He began to work for His uncles in their trading business. Those same qualities that had set Him apart from other children, His dignity, His truthfulness, His sweetness of character and His humility, made Him a well-respected merchant. He was always scrupulously fair, He was attentive to every small detail of business and He never cheated anyone.

When He was sixteen the Báb went to work in Búshihr, as His uncles had a branch of their business in that busy port. The Báb worked in Búshihr as He had in Shíráz, with care and precision; he was attentive to His religious duties and He gave large sums of money to charity. At this time, Khadíjih-Bagum, who was living quietly at home in Shíráz, dreamed one night of the Báb. She saw Him standing in a green and flower-covered plain and facing towards Mecca in an attitude of prayer. His face was radiant and He wore an outer coat on which verses from the Holy Qur'án were embroidered with threads of gold. In the morning, Khadíjih-Bagum told her mother and the mother and grandmother of the Báb of this vivid and beautiful dream. They all assured her that it was the Báb's devoted attention to His prayers that had enabled her to see Him in a dream.

During the years that the Báb lived in Búshihr, He spent many hours in prayer. Every morning, as the sun rose over the flat, white roofs of the city, He turned in prayer in the direction of Ṭihrán and chanted words of praise and glorification of God, and every Friday He spent several hours in prayer and meditation.

When the Báb was twenty He took over entire responsibility for the running of His uncles' business in Búshihr. Two years later, in 1841, He wrote a letter to His uncles requesting their permission to go on a pilgrimage to the holy cities of Najaf and Karbilá. The Báb longed to make a pilgrimage but His uncles were slow to reply to his letter. The Báb brought all outstanding business matters up to date, put all the account books in order and closed the office. He left the keys with a trustworthy person in Búshihr, wrote to His uncles telling them what He had done and set out on pilgrimage.

The Báb spent several months in Karbilá and Najaf and passed many hours at the thresholds of the holy shrines. He would stand in an attitude of prayer at the doorway of the shrine of the Imám Ḥusayn, so wrapt in His devotions that He seemed utterly oblivious of all around Him. Tears rained from His eyes and the words 'O God, my God, my Beloved, my heart's Desire' fell from His lips. Those visiting pilgrims who were near enough to hear Him instinctively interrupted their own devotions and marvelled at His youthful devotion and piety. When He had completed His prayers, He did not cross the threshold of the shrine or attempt to address anyone around Him but returned quietly to His home.

Siyyid Káẓim knew of the Báb's presence in Karbilá, for one day, at dawn, he sent a messenger to fetch to his home a student named Shaykh Ḥasan-i-Zunúzí.

'A highly esteemed and distinguished Person has arrived,' Siyyid Káẓim told Shaykh Ḥasan; 'I feel it incumbent upon us both to visit Him.'

The morning light was just breaking as they went quietly

through the narrow streets of Karbilá to a certain house where the Báb stood at the doorway waiting to receive them. He quietly approached them and then held out His arms to Siyyid Káẓim and embraced him. Siyyid Káẓim then stood speechless and with bowed head before the Báb in an attitude of profound reverence while the Báb spoke to him with great kindness, affection and respect. The Báb also greeted Shaykh Ḥasan in a kindly manner and soon led both His guests to the upper floor of the house. He showed them into a beautiful room that was fragrant with vases of sweet-scented flowers and invited them to be seated. Siyyid Káẓim and Shaykh Ḥasan sat down on the carpeted floor but they scarcely knew what they were doing, so overpowering was the sense of delight which had seized them both.

In the very centre of the room was a beautiful silver cup. According to the teachings of Islám, the followers of Muḥammad are forbidden to drink from such a cup, but soon after they entered the room the Báb filled this cup to overflowing and gave it to Siyyid Káẓim, quoting as He did so a verse from the Holy Qur'án: '*A drink of a pure beverage shall their Lord give them.*'

Shaykh Ḥasan watched with amazement as Siyyid Káẓim took the cup in both hands and drank from it. He then returned the cup to the Báb reverently and the Báb offered it to Shaykh Ḥasan though He did not speak to him. Shaykh Ḥasan could see that Siyyid Káẓim was filled with a reverent joy which he could not suppress. He himself was struck with wonder at the charm and dignity of the Báb, at the cordial welcome they were both given and at the delicious fragrance of the drink they were offered. No other words were spoken and the Báb soon rose, accompanied His guests to the door and bade them a kind farewell. Siyyid Káẓim and Shaykh Ḥasan went their separate ways home and Siyyid Káẓim offered no explanation to his pupil of this strange and joyful encounter.

Three days later, Shaykh Ḥasan was seated at a lecture being given by Siyyid Káẓim when he saw the Báb, of whose name and identity he still knew nothing, arrive in the room where Siyyid Káẓim was addressing his disciples. The Báb took a seat close to the front of the group and listened with modesty and dignity to what was being said. As soon as Siyyid Káẓim saw who had entered the room and was seated in his class, he stopped speaking. In the silence that followed, one of his students begged him to resume the argument that he had left unfinished.

'What more shall I say?' Siyyid Káẓim asked and turned his face towards the Báb. At that very moment, a shaft of sunlight streamed through a window directly onto the Báb as He sat at the feet of Siyyid Káẓim.

'Lo,' said Siyyid Káẓim, 'the Truth is more manifest than the ray of light that has fallen upon that lap.'

'Why is it', asked the student who had spoken before, 'that you neither reveal His name nor identify His person?' Siyyid Káẓim gave no words in answer, but replied by pointing with his finger to his own throat, implying that were he to divulge His name, they would both be killed instantly.

The Báb's mother began to be anxious at His long absence in the holy cities and sent Ḥájí Mírzá Siyyid 'Alí to Iráq to ask Him to return to Shíráz. He did as she asked and returned home but He soon expressed a wish to visit Najaf and Karbilá again. At this His mother became somewhat alarmed and she sought the help of her brothers in arranging a marriage for her son.

One night at this time, the sweet and gentle young cousin of the Báb, Khadíjih-Bagum, dreamed that Fáṭimih, the daughter of the Prophet Muḥammad, came to ask for her hand in marriage to the Imám Ḥusayn. In the morning she told her mother of this dream and her mother became very happy. That same day, the mother and the grandmother of the Báb came to call on the mother of Khadíjih-Bagum and they requested that a marriage be arranged between the two young cousins. The marriage took place two months later, in August 1842, and it was celebrated with marriage feasts in both houses.

The Báb and Khadíjih-Bagum began a quiet married life together. The Báb's mother lived with them and they employed two servants. The Báb and Khadíjih-Bagum were very happy together and Khadíjih-Bagum felt herself to be most fortunate. But not long after their marriage she had a most terrifying dream. She dreamed that there was a large and fearsome lion in the courtyard of their house and that she had her arms around the neck of the lion. She could not get away from the beast and it dragged her twice right around the courtyard of the house and once more around half of the courtyard. Khadíjih-Bagum woke up feeling very frightened. She related this dream to the Báb and He explained to her that the dream foretold that their life together would not last for more than two and a half years. Khadíjih-Bagum was greatly troubled and distressed at hearing this but the Báb spoke to her calmly with words of love and comfort and helped her to be ready to accept every adversity in the path of God.

Some time in the year 1843 the Báb Himself had a significant dream which He described in later years in the following words:

'In My vision I saw the head of the Imám Ḥusayn, the Siyyidu'sh-Shuhadá', which was hanging upon a tree. Drops of blood dripped profusely from His lacerated throat. With feelings of unsurpassed delight, I approached that tree and, stretching forth My hands, gathered a few drops of that sacred blood, and drank them devoutly. When I awoke, I felt that the Spirit of God had permeated and taken possession of My soul. My heart was thrilled with the joy of His Divine presence, and the mysteries of His revelation were unfolded before My eyes in all their glory.'

The Báb further explained that the spirit of prayer which animated His soul and guided His actions from that day onwards was the direct consequence of this dream. He understood from it that God wished Him to convey a message of tremendous importance to the peoples of the world.

In 1843 a son was born to the Báb and Khadíjih-Bagum. Khadíjih-Bagum was dangerously ill at the time of delivery; both her own life and the life of the child were in danger. The mother of the Báb told her Son that His wife was on the point of death and that the child was not yet born. The Báb took up a mirror and wrote a prayer on it. He told His mother to hold the mirror in front of His wife. When that was done Khadíjih-Bagum was delivered of the child, but the infant, a boy whom his parents named Aḥmad, was either stillborn or died shortly after his birth. The Báb comforted Khadíjih-Bagum as they grieved together in their great loss, and later wrote the following words of consolation for her:

'O well-beloved! Value highly the grace of the Great Remembrance for it cometh from God, the Loved One. Thou shalt not be a woman, like other women, if thou obeyest God in the Cause of Truth, the greatest Truth. Know thou the great bounty conferred upon thee by the Ancient of Days, and take pride in being the consort of the Well-Beloved, Who is loved by God, the Greatest. Sufficient unto thee is this glory which cometh unto thee from God, the All-Wise, the All-Praised. Be patient in all that God hath ordained concerning the Báb and His Family. Verily, thy son, Aḥmad, is with Fáṭimih, the Sublime, in the sanctified Paradise.'

The Báb revealed the following prayer on the death of Aḥmad:

'O My God, My only Desire! Grant that the sacrifice of My son, My only son, may be acceptable unto Thee. Grant that it be a prelude to the sacrifice of My own, My entire self, in the path of Thy good pleasure. Endue with Thy grace My life-blood which I yearn to shed in Thy path. Cause it to water and nourish the seed of Thy Faith. Endow it with Thy celestial potency, that this infant seed of God may soon germinate in the hearts of men, that it may thrive and prosper, that it may grow to become a mighty tree, beneath the shadow of which all the peoples and kindreds of the earth may gather. Answer Thou My prayer, O God, and fulfil My most cherished desire. Thou art, verily, the Almighty, the All-Bountiful.'

The Báb's mother was deeply grieved and angry at the loss of Aḥmad. She remonstrated with her Son, saying that if He had such power that He could save the life of His wife when she was on the point of death, why could He not also have saved the life of His son and spared His wife so much suffering. The Báb told His mother that He was destined to leave no children to survive Him. This reply made His mother even more angry, but although she continued to reproach Him, the Báb would say no more.

CHAPTER 3

'O WELL-BELOVED'

At this time in His life the Báb had no definite occupation and spent much of His time at prayer in the upper room of the house. Some mornings He walked in the fields outside the city, returning home only at sunset.

One afternoon He came home from a walk earlier than usual, informed Khadíjih-Bagum that He had a particular task to attend to that evening and asked that the evening meal be served early. After their meal, the Báb went to bed and slept. Khadíjih-Bagum also slept, but about an hour later, when the house was quiet, she heard her husband get up and leave their room. When He had not returned one hour later, Khadíjih-Bagum became anxious and got up to search for Him. She thought that He might have left the house, but she found the main door locked from the inside and knew that He must be still inside the house. She walked to the western side of the house and looked up to the rooftop. She saw, to her surprise, that there was a light burning in the upper room. Khadíjih-Bagum knew that the Báb never went to that part of the house at night unless He had guests.

Khadíjih-Bagum climbed the steps at the northern side of the courtyard, wondering what might have taken Him to that room. Then she caught sight of Him standing in the room. His face was luminous and it seemed to her that rays of light streamed from it. Tears streamed from His eyes. His hands were raised and He was chanting a prayer in a most melodious voice.

Khadíjih-Bagum trembled with fright as she looked at

Him. She was unable either to enter the room or retreat. It seemed to her that she had no will of her own and she felt herself on the point of screaming when the Báb motioned to her indicating that she should go back down the stairs. She then found that she had enough courage to return to her bed but she could not sleep. She lay there until the morning, wondering what might have happened to cause such tears and sorrow and to induce prayers and supplications of such intensity.

In the morning, when the sun rose, their servant took the samovar to the room of the Báb's mother and the Báb went there as usual to drink tea. Khadíjih-Bagum followed Him. His mother had left he room. When Khadíjih-Bagum looked at her husband, she saw in Him, once again, the same majesty and splendour that she had witnessed the previous night. She grew pale and began to shake with terror.

The Báb greeted her with great kindness and affection. He asked her to sit down and gave her tea to drink from His own cup. Khadíjih-Bagum felt her strength and courage returning and when the Báb asked her what troubled her, she was able to say that it was the great change in Him that she had witnessed during the night. The Báb smiled at her and said that, although He had not wished to be seen in the upper room, God had ordained otherwise. He explained that it was the Will of God that she should see Him in that way so that she should come to know with absolute certitude that He was a Manifestation of God.

As soon as she heard these words, Khadíjih-Bagum believed in Him and her heart became calm and assured. She fell on her face before Him and from that moment on she lived only to serve Him. The Báb did all that He could to strengthen and prepare her for the ordeals that lay ahead.

CHAPTER 4

MULLÁ ḤUSAYN REACHES SHÍRÁZ

Around the same time that the Báb's baby son, Aḥmad, died in Shíráz, Siyyid Káẓim passed away in Karbilá and Mullá Ḥusayn set out with his two companions on his search for the Promised One.

On leaving Karbilá, Mullá Ḥusayn and his two companions, his brother and his nephew, went first to Najaf to pray at the shrines and then went directly south to the port of Búshihr where the Báb had recently lived and worked.

In Búshihr Mullá Ḥusayn felt his heart stir with hope and longing, for the presence of the Báb in that town and the prayers that He had said while there had changed the very air of the place and Mullá Ḥusayn's pure heart was able to detect the holy fragrance. While Mullá Ḥusayn felt this new stirring of hope, he knew that he must not stay long in Búshihr, so he and his companions pushed on north-eastwards across the desert to Shíráz, following the route that Shaykh Aḥmad had taken many years before. Mullá Ḥusayn was drawn irresistibly through the dry hills to Shíráz.

On the evening of 22 May 1844 the three young men arrived at the gate of the city of Shíráz; they were hot, dusty, tired and hungry. The city lay before them, the beautiful domes of its mosques glimmering above the walls and the tops of cypresses and pine trees promising shade and the sweet scents of roses and jasmine. Mullá Ḥusayn lingered outside the city gate and then sent his companions ahead of him into the city asking them to wait for him at the mosque and telling them that he would join them there for evening prayers.

When he was alone, he walked and prayed by himself near the gate of the city, beseeching God with all his heart to lead him to the Promised One. As he walked and prayed, he saw a youth of the city coming towards him. The young man wore a green turban – a sign that He was descended from the Prophet Muḥammad – and His face was radiant with joy. He came towards Mullá Ḥusayn, greeted him with a smile of loving welcome and embraced him as if he were His own long-lost brother.

Mullá Ḥusayn thought at first that the youth must be a disciple of Siyyid Káẓim who had somehow heard of his arrival and was coming out to meet him. The young man was 'Alí-Muḥammad, the Báb, and He invited Mullá Ḥusayn to come to His own house and refresh himself after his journey. Mullá Ḥusayn explained that his brother and nephew were waiting for him at the mosque.

'Commit them to the care of God,' said the Báb. 'He will surely protect and watch over them.'

The Báb was so courteous and so firm that Mullá Ḥusayn felt himself unable to refuse the invitation and he followed Him into the city. The gentle dignity of the Báb, the charm of His voice, the very way that He walked, all made Mullá Ḥusayn marvellously happy to be with Him.

They reached a modest house in a quiet corner of the city, the door of which was opened by an Ethiopian servant. As the Báb entered His house, He spoke a few words which Mullá Ḥusayn recognised as being from the Holy Qur'án – '*Enter therein in peace, secure*', and he felt the power and majesty in those words enter his very soul.

Silently Mullá Ḥusayn followed his host into the house and the feeling of joyful wonder that had overtaken him as he walked with the Báb into the city increased with every step that he now took. He felt that this meeting must lead him, in some way, a step nearer to finding the One he sought.

CHAPTER 5
THE BÁB DECLARES HIS MISSION

Once they were inside the house, the Báb led the way to an upper room, invited Mullá Ḥusayn to sit down and called for water to be brought. He Himself poured the water over the hands of His guest and then called for the samovar and Himself prepared the tea. While they drank tea together Mullá Ḥusayn felt that his body and spirit were being marvellously refreshed and strengthened. When the tea was finished, he felt that he must go and find his companions, and he got to his feet.

'The time for evening prayer is approaching,' he said; 'I have promised my friends to join them at that hour.'

The Báb answered calmly and with great courtesy.

'You must surely have made the hour of your return conditional upon the will and pleasure of God. It seems that His will has decreed otherwise. You need have no fear of having broken your pledge.'

Mullá Ḥusayn did not know what to reply. He still thought of his two companions waiting for him, but the confidence of the Báb calmed his mind so he prepared himself to say his evening prayers there in that house.

While Mullá Ḥusayn and the Báb said their prayers together, Mullá Ḥusayn prayed with all his heart for God's guidance. The strain and stress of his search was heavy on his heart and he could not understand the purpose of the present mysterious encounter. He breathed this silent prayer:

'I have striven with all my soul, O my God, and until now have failed to find Thy promised Messenger. I testify that

Thy word faileth not, and that Thy promise is sure.'

When the prayers were finished, the Báb invited Mullá Ḥusayn to sit and talk with Him. It was about one hour after sunset when the Báb began to question Mullá Ḥusayn about his journey. Mullá Ḥusayn explained that he was a student of the late Siyyid Káẓim and that he was searching for the Promised One. The Báb asked:

'Whom, after Siyyid Káẓim, do you regard as his successor and your leader?'

Mullá Ḥusayn replied:

'At the hour of his death, our departed teacher insistently exhorted us to forsake our homes, to scatter far and wide, in quest of the promised Beloved. I have, accordingly, journeyed to Persia, have arisen to accomplish his will and am still engaged in my quest.'

'Has your teacher', asked the Báb, 'given you any detailed indications as to the distinguishing features of the Promised One?'

'Yes,' replied Mullá Ḥusayn. 'He is of a pure lineage, is of illustrious descent and of the seed of Fáṭimih. As to His age, He is more than twenty and less than thirty. He is endowed with innate knowledge, He is of medium height, abstains from smoking and is free from bodily deficiency.'

The Báb paused for a while and then, in a vibrant voice, He declared:

'Behold, all these signs are manifest in Me.'

Mullá Ḥusayn was startled and felt that the room about him was filled with a mysterious spiritual power. He did not speak and the Báb spoke again. He explained to Mullá Ḥusayn how each one of those signs could be seen in Him. Mullá Ḥusayn was shocked. He said:

'He whose advent we await is a Man of unsurpassed holiness, and the Cause He is to reveal, a Cause of tremendous power.'

As soon as these words were spoken, Mullá Ḥusayn was seized with fear but he could not think why he should be so afraid. When his fear abated, he decided that he would humbly ask his host to look at a paper that he was carrying with him. While in Karbilá, Mullá Ḥusayn had drawn up a list of questions relating to the teachings of Shaykh Aḥmad and Siyyid Káẓim. He had not yet found anyone who could explain certain aspects of their teachings to him. He was carrying this list with him and he now determined to show it to the Báb.

Mullá Ḥusayn also remembered something that Siyyid Káẓim had told him. There is one very difficult chapter in the Holy Qur'án which is called the Súrih of Joseph. Mullá Ḥusayn had once asked Siyyid Káẓim to explain the meaning of the Súrih of Joseph to him and Siyyid Káẓim had replied:

'This is, verily, beyond me. He, that great One, who comes after me will, unasked, reveal it for you.'

While Mullá Ḥusayn was turning these things over in his mind, the Báb spoke again.

'Observe attentively,' He said. 'Might not the Person intended by Siyyid Káẓim be none other than I?'

Mullá Ḥusayn then asked the Báb to look at the questions he had written.

'Will you,' he asked, 'read this book of mine and look at its pages with indulgent eyes? I pray you to overlook my weaknesses and failings.'

The Báb took the book, opened it, glanced at certain passages, closed it and began to speak. Within a few minutes He had answered all the questions to Mullá Ḥusayn's complete satisfaction. He then went on to explain certain spiritual truths which Mullá Ḥusayn had never heard spoken of before. Mullá Ḥusayn listened in silent amazement, wondering at the life and power in the words spoken by the

Báb. When He had completed these explanations the Báb spoke again.

'Had you not been My guest,' He told Mullá Ḥusayn, 'your position would indeed have been a grievous one. The all-encompassing grace of God has saved you. It is for God to test His servants, and not for His servants to judge Him in accordance with their deficient standards. Were I to fail to resolve your perplexities, could the Reality that shines within Me be regarded as powerless, or My knowledge be accused as faulty? Nay, by the righteousness of God! it behoves, in this day, the peoples and nations of both the East and the West to hasten to this threshold, and here seek to obtain the reviving grace of the Merciful . . . It behoves them to arise, as earnestly and spontaneously as you have arisen, and to seek with determination and constancy their promised Beloved.'

The Báb then said, to Mullá Ḥusayn's wonder and amazement:

'Now is the time to reveal the commentary on the Súrih of Joseph.'

He took up His pen and began to write very quickly in an exquisitely fine hand, and as He wrote He chanted aloud:

'All praise be to God Who hath, through the power of Truth, sent down this Book unto His servant, that it may serve as a shining light for all mankind . . . Verily this is none other than the sovereign Truth; it is the Path which God hath laid out for all that are in heaven and on earth . . . This is indeed the eternal Truth which God, the Ancient of Days, hath revealed unto His omnipotent Word . . . This is the Mystery which hath been hidden from all that are in heaven and on earth . . .'

Mullá Ḥusayn was enthralled by the beauty of the Báb's voice and by the power of the words He uttered. He had never seen anyone write so fast or so beautifully before. He was enraptured by all that he heard and saw. The Báb continued to write and to chant and Mullá Ḥusayn continued to listen while the Báb revealed and wrote, with incredible rapidity, the entire first chapter of His commentary on the Súrih of Joseph, which we now know as one of His most famous books, the Qayyumu'l-Asmá'.

Mullá Ḥusayn then remembered that his brother and his nephew were waiting for him at the mosque. He got to his feet and asked the Báb if he might leave.

'If you leave in such a state,' replied the Báb, 'whoever sees you will assuredly say: "this poor youth has lost his mind".'

Mullá Ḥusayn took his seat again. It was just two hours after sunset.

'This night,' the Báb declared, 'this very hour will, in the days to come, be celebrated as one of the greatest and most significant of all festivals. Render thanks to God for having graciously assisted you to attain your heart's desire . . .'

He continued to share with Mullá Ḥusayn his joy and exaltation that the long-awaited day of peace and justice for all peoples had finally dawned. Three hours after sunset, the Báb called for dinner to be served and the same Ethiopian servant who had opened the door of the house for them earlier in the evening now came and served them a most delicious meal. The food refreshed Mullá Ḥusayn's tired body and brought new strength to him. He felt as if he must indeed be in paradise for he had never in his life been so happy. After they had eaten, the Báb spoke again, explaining further to Mullá Ḥusayn the significance of His declaration.

In the Qayyumu'l-Asmá' the Báb explains that God has created Him to convey a message to all the peoples of the earth:

'Out of utter nothingness, O great and omnipotent Master, Thou hast, through the celestial potency of Thy might, brought me forth and raised me up to proclaim this Revelation.'

In this same book, the Báb claims that He is 'none other than the mighty Word of God' and states that He is 'none other than the Promised One Himself, invested with the power of the sovereign Truth'.

He specifically addresses the people of Persia:

'O people of Persia! . . . Verily ye have been especially favoured by God through this mighty Word. Then do not withdraw from the sanctuary of His presence, for, by the righteousness of the One true God, He is none other than the sovereign Truth from God; He is the most exalted One and the Source of all wisdom . . .'

His message is, however, for all the peoples of the world. He writes:

'O ye peoples of the earth! Hearken unto My call . . . Enter ye, one and all, through this Gate . . .'

Referring to Himself as 'His Remembrance', the Báb declares:

'O peoples of the earth! Verily His Remembrance is come to you from God after an interval during which there were no Messengers, that He may purge and purify you from uncleanliness in anticipation of the Day of the One true God . . .'

Mullá Ḥusayn later described that momentous night of 22 May 1844 in these words:

'I sat spellbound by His utterance, oblivious of time and of those who awaited me . . . Sleep had departed from me that night. I was enthralled by the music of that voice which rose and fell as He chanted . . . All the delights, all the ineffable glories, which the Almighty has recounted in His Book as the priceless possessions of the people of Paradise, these I seemed to be experiencing that night.'

Suddenly there was a sound from outside the house. The city stirred and woke as the call from the minarets summoned the faithful Muslims to their morning prayers. This call awakened Mullá Ḥusayn from his state of ecstasy. The Báb addressed him in these words:

'O thou who art the first to believe in Me! Verily I say, I am the Báb, the Gate of God, and thou art the Bábu'l-Báb, the gate of that Gate. Eighteen souls must, in the beginning, spontaneously and of their own accord, accept Me and recognise the truth of My Revelation. Unwarned and uninvited each of these must seek independently to find Me.'

He then told Mullá Ḥusayn not to share with anyone what he had seen and heard but to go back to his companions and continue with his teaching as if nothing had happened. Accompanying Mullá Ḥusayn to the door of His house, He committed him to the care of God.

Mullá Ḥusayn did exactly as the Báb instructed him. He went and found his companions, began to organise some classes in the city and told no one his tremendous secret. But he knew that his own life would never be the same again; this is how he describes the effect upon him of the Báb's declaration:

'This Revelation, so suddenly and impetuously thrust upon me, came as a thunderbolt which, for a time, seemed to have benumbed my faculties. I was blinded by its dazzling splendour and overwhelmed by its crushing force. Excitement, joy, awe and wonder stirred the depths of my soul. Predominant among these emotions was a sense of gladness and strength which seemed to have transfigured me. How feeble and impotent, how dejected and timid, I had felt previously! Then I could neither write nor walk, so tremulous were my hands and feet. Now, however, the knowledge of His Revelation had galvanised my being. I felt possessed of such courage and power that were the world, all its people and its potentates, to rise against me, I would, alone and undaunted, withstand their onslaught. The universe seemed but a handful of dust in my grasp. I seemed to be the Voice of Gabriel personified, calling unto all mankind:

'Awake, for, lo! the morning Light has broken. Arise, for His Cause is made manifest. The portal of His grace is open wide; enter therein, O peoples of the world! For He Who is your Promised One is come!'

All alone, amongst the many millions of the world's peoples, Mullá Ḥusayn knew that God's promises to humanity were being fulfilled and that the long-awaited day of peace had, at last, dawned. Rejoicing in his innermost being, his heart brimming with praise and gratitude and his face radiating light and happiness, Mullá Ḥusayn kept in his heart the secret of the Báb's declaration. He prayed eagerly and earnestly that the time would soon come when he would be able to share with others these joyous tidings.

II

Raising the Call of a New Day

1844

CHAPTER 6
THE LETTERS OF THE LIVING

When Mullá Ḥusayn began to teach as the Báb had instructed him, many people came to hear him, amongst them some leaders of religion and some important citizens of Shíráz. He told no one his secret, but the joy and confidence he now felt shone in his face and he attracted many listeners. On several occasions the Báb sent His Ethiopian servant at night to fetch Mullá Ḥusayn to His house.

'Every time I visited Him', Mullá Ḥusayn wrote, 'I spent the entire night in His presence. Wakeful until the dawn, I sat at His feet fascinated by the charm of His utterance and oblivious of the world and its cares and pursuits. How rapidly those precious hours flew by!'

One night the Báb said to Mullá Ḥusayn:

'Tomorrow thirteen of your companions will arrive. To each of them extend the utmost loving-kindness. Leave them not to themselves, for they have dedicated their lives to the quest of their Beloved. Pray to God that He may graciously enable them to walk securely in that path which is finer than a hair and keener than a sword.'

The very same morning, at sunrise, just as Mullá Ḥusayn reached his own house, Mullá 'Alí and twelve other students of Siyyid Káẓim arrived in Shíráz. Mullá Ḥusayn greeted them joyfully and found somewhere for them to stay. It was very difficult for him to keep his great secret to himself but he obeyed the Báb and said not a word to them about the Promised One. However, they could all see that something wonderful had happened to Mullá Ḥusayn. He was so full of joy, so very different from the Mullá Ḥusayn they had known in Karbilá. After three days, Mullá 'Alí could bear it no longer and he begged Mullá Ḥusayn to tell him the secret of his great happiness. During their conversation, Mullá 'Alí understood that Mullá Ḥusayn had indeed found the One they all sought and he implored Mullá Ḥusayn to tell him who He was.

'Beseech me not to grant you this favour,' Mullá Ḥusayn replied. 'Let your trust be in Him, for He will surely guide your steps . . .'

Mullá 'Alí hurried back to his twelve companions and told them what he had learnt. His account of his conversation with Mullá Ḥusayn filled all their hearts with fresh hope and longing. Each of them went to his own room to pray and fast. Here is one of the prayers they prayed:

'O God, our God! Thee only do we worship and to Thee do we cry for help. Guide us, we beseech Thee, on the straight Path, O Lord our God! . . . Verily, Thou wilt not break Thy promise.'

Mullá 'Alí and his companions spent three nights in prayer and fasting and on the third night, while he prayed, Mullá 'Alí saw in a vision a bright light. It moved ahead of him and as he followed it with his eyes, it led him to see, in beauty and splendour, the face of the Báb. Exultant with joy and radiant with gladness, he flung open the door of his room, ran to find Mullá Ḥusayn and threw himself into his friend's arms. Mullá Ḥusayn embraced him lovingly and said:

'Praise be to God who hath guided us hither.'

At daybreak Mullá Ḥusayn and Mullá 'Alí hurried together to the house of the Báb. At the entrance to the house the Báb's servant was waiting to welcome them. He told them that the Báb had told him to expect two guests in the early morning and he took them to the upper room where the Báb welcomed them. This time there were no questions, for there was no possibility of doubt and the very room in which they sat seemed to be filled with the power of God.

One by one, the twelve companions of Mullá 'Alí, independently of one another, came to recognise the Báb. Some saw a vision of the Báb while asleep or at the moment of waking and some saw Him while at prayer. All were led to the presence of the Báb and were enrolled as His first disciples. The Báb gave them the title 'Letters of the Living'. Altogether eighteen people, independently and unaided, recognised the Báb.

There was one woman amongst the Letters of the Living. We know her as Ṭáhirih, a name later given to her by the Báb. She never met the Báb but she saw a vision of Him in a dream and became His disciple. Ṭáhirih was an exceptionally beautiful and gifted woman: she was brilliantly clever and utterly fearless. She had become a student of Siyyid Káẓim in spite of fierce opposition from her husband and family, and had travelled to Karbilá in the hope of meeting him but arrived shortly after he died. One of the twelve companions of Mullá 'Alí was the brother-in-law of Ṭáhirih. He carried with him a letter from her in which she expressed her belief in the Promised One.

The last of the Letters of the Living to arrive was Muḥammad-'Alí of Barfurúsh, who is known as Quddús, a name later given to him by the Báb. He was the youngest of the Báb's disciples. This is the story of how Quddús found the Báb.

One night, the Báb spoke these words to Mullá Ḥusayn:

'Seventeen Letters have thus far enlisted under the standard of the Faith of God. There remains one more to complete the number. These Letters of the Living shall arise to proclaim My Cause and to establish My Faith. Tomorrow night the remaining Letter will arrive and will complete the number of My chosen disciples.'

During the evening of the next day, as the Báb was returning to His house with Mullá Ḥusayn, they saw a young man, dusty and travel-stained, approaching them. The young man saw Mullá Ḥusayn first and rushed to greet him. He was Quddús. Quddús had become a student of Siyyid Káẓim during the last years of the Siyyid's life, and his modesty and lowliness had distinguished him amongst the Siyyid's disciples. He was just twenty-two years old when he reached Shíráz, led, like Mullá Ḥusayn, by the guidance of God.

Quddús at once asked Mullá Ḥusayn if he had found the Promised One. Mullá Ḥusayn tried to calm his agitation and promised that he would speak with him later, but just then Quddús caught sight of the Báb. He could not take his eyes from the figure of the Báb.

'Why seek you to hide Him from me?' he cried out to Mullá Ḥusayn. 'I can recognise Him by His gait. I confidently testify that none besides Him, whether in the East or in the West, can claim to be the Truth. None other can manifest the power and majesty that radiate from His holy person.'

Mullá Ḥusayn was astonished. He told Quddús that he would soon explain everything to him, begged him to wait a while and hurried after the Báb. When he explained to the Báb what had happened, he was told:

'Marvel not at his strange behaviour. We have in the world of the spirit been communing with that youth. We know him already. We indeed awaited his coming. Go to him and summon him forthwith to Our presence.'

CHAPTER 7
'ARISE IN HIS NAME'

Mullá Ḥusayn took Quddús to the house of the Báb where the Báb welcomed him lovingly. Very soon after this, the Báb called Mullá Ḥusayn to Him and said: 'The days of our companionship are approaching their end.'

He said, 'Gird up the loins of endeavour and arise to diffuse My Cause. Be not dismayed at the sight of the degeneracy and perversity of this generation, for the Lord of the Covenant shall assuredly assist you. Verily, He shall surround you with His loving protection, and shall lead you from victory to victory. Even as the cloud that rains its bounty upon the earth, traverse the land from end to end and shower upon its people the blessings which the Almighty, in His mercy, has deigned to confer upon you . . . Those whom you find receptive to your call, share with them the epistles and tablets We have revealed for you, that, perchance, these wondrous words may cause them to turn away from the slough of heedlessness, and soar into the realm of the Divine presence.'

Mullá Ḥusayn knew that the Báb intended to make a pilgrimage to Mecca. He longed to be allowed to accompany Him, but the Báb told him that He planned to take Quddús with Him to Mecca. Mullá Ḥusayn was disappointed but the Báb assured him that he had been given a most important task to accomplish. He asked Mullá Ḥusayn to start on a journey northwards to spread the new teachings.

The Báb made it clear that Mullá Ḥusayn had a very

special mission to Ṭihrán but He did not say exactly what it was.

'Beseech almighty Providence', He said to Mullá Ḥusayn, 'that He may graciously enable you to attain, in that capital, the seat of true sovereignty, and to enter the mansion of the Beloved. A secret lies hidden in that city. When made manifest, it shall turn the earth into paradise. My hope is that you may partake of its grace and recognise its splendour.'

The Báb then called Mullá 'Alí to him and told him to go and teach in Iráq. He instructed Mullá 'Alí not to reveal His identity but to share with everyone the news that He had declared His mission.

'Your faith', He said, 'must be immovable as the rock, must weather every storm and survive every calamity. You are the first to leave the House of God, and to suffer for His sake. If you be slain in His path, remember that great will be your reward, and goodly the gift which will be bestowed upon you.'

Having given this mission to Mullá 'Alí, the Báb called to Him the other Letters of the Living present and gave to each a special task. He instructed them all to record the name of every believer who embraced the Faith and identified himself with the teachings. He asked them to send the names in sealed letters to His uncle, Ḥájí Mírzá Siyyid 'Alí, who would deliver them to Him.

'Of all these believers', He said, 'I shall make mention in the Tablet of God, so that upon each one of them the Beloved of our hearts may, in the Day when He shall have ascended the throne of glory, confer His inestimable blessings, and declare them the dwellers of His Paradise.'

He addressed them all with these parting words:

'O My beloved friends! You are the bearers of the name of God in this Day. You have been chosen as the repositories of His mystery. It behoves each one of you to manifest the attributes of God, and to exemplify by your deeds and words the signs of His righteousness, His power and glory. The very members of your body must bear witness to the loftiness of your purpose, the integrity of your life, the reality of your faith, and the exalted character of your devotion . . . You are the first Letters that have been generated from the Primal Point, the first Springs that have welled out from the Source of this Revelation. Beseech the Lord your God to grant that no earthly entanglements, no worldly affections, no ephemeral pursuits, may tarnish the purity, or embitter the sweetness, of that grace which flows through you. I am preparing you for the advent of a mighty Day. Exert your utmost endeavour that, in the world to come, I, who am now instructing you, may, before the mercy-seat of God, rejoice in your deeds and glory in your achievements . . . Scatter throughout the length and breadth of this land, and, with steadfast feet and sanctified hearts, prepare the way for His coming. Heed not your weaknesses and frailty, fix your gaze upon the invincible power of the Lord, your God, the Almighty . . . Arise in His name, put your trust wholly in Him, and be assured of ultimate victory.'

Early one morning while the streets of the city were still dark, the Letters of the Living, all who had reached Shíráz except Mullá Ḥusayn and Quddús, left the city and set out to spread the news of the coming of the Báb.

CHAPTER 8

THE FIRST TO SUFFER

Mullá 'Alí set out eagerly to share the news of the coming of the Báb but he was severely beaten even before he left Shíráz by one of the city's most prominent citizens who accused him of leading his son astray. This experience showed him how steep and difficult was the path ahead of him but he went, as directed by the Báb, back to Iráq, retracing the steps which he had earlier taken in quest of God's new Messenger. In Karbilá he joyfully met with Ṭáhirih.

Mullá 'Alí took with him to Iráq a copy of the book which the Báb had revealed on the night He declared His mission, the commentary on the Súrih of Joseph. He gave this and other writings of the Báb to the divines of Karbilá. The news aroused eager interest amongst many people in the city. The disciples of Siyyid Káẓim were in a fairly strong position in Karbilá, as there were a good number of them. Several people responded swiftly to the message that Mullá 'Alí brought and believed in the Báb. When the divines saw this happening, they began to oppose Mullá 'Alí.

From Karbilá Mullá 'Alí went to Najaf, where there were only a few followers of Shaykh Aḥmad and Siyyid Káẓim. In the face of a large gathering, Mullá 'Alí fearlessly announced the news of the appearance of the Báb to one of the leading religious dignitaries of the city.

'His proof,' he declared, 'is His Word; His testimony, none other than the testimony with which Islám seeks to vindicate its truth. From the pen of this unschooled Háshimite Youth of Persia there have streamed, within the space of forty-eight hours, as great a number of verses, of prayers, of homilies and scientific treatises, as would equal in volume the whole of the Qur'án, which it took Muḥammad, the Prophet of God, twenty-three years to reveal!'

The distinguished cleric to whom he addressed these words immediately pronounced Mullá 'Alí a heretic and threw him out of the meeting. His disciples also condemned Mullá 'Alí and joined with other leading Shí'ite divines in order to rid themselves of this new heresy. Even the followers of Shaykh Aḥmad and Siyyid Káẓim joined in the general condemnation, although they knew of Mullá 'Alí's piety, sincerity and great learning. The divines of Najaf handed Mullá 'Alí over to the Ottoman official in the city, calling him a wrecker of Islám, a disgrace to their Faith and a mischief-maker deserving of death.

They sent him north to Baghdád, the old and famous city on the river Tigris which was the regional centre of the Ottoman administration in that area.

The governor of Baghdád ordered that his books be taken from him and put in the council-chamber and that he be thrown into prison. From his prison cell, Mullá 'Alí continued to teach all with whom he came in contact. As a result of his teaching the Cause of the Báb grew day by day in Baghdád. When the authorities and the religious leaders saw what was happening, they became alarmed. An assembly of divines, many of them of the Sunní sect of Islám, summoned Mullá 'Alí to appear before them. They brought him out from the prison and as he stood before them, they asked him Who the Lord of his Cause was. He answered:

'The awaited Spirit of Truth has come. He is the One promised in the Books of God.'

He then read them some verses and prayers of the Báb and called on them to believe. With scornful pride, the divines rejected his message and condemned him to death. The governor sent a report of what had happened to Constantinople, the capital of the Ottoman Empire, and orders came back that Mullá 'Alí should be brought with his books to Constantinople. After being imprisoned for six months in Baghdád, Mullá 'Alí began the long journey.

He reached Constantinople, but after the severe privations of his imprisonment in Baghdád the strain was too much for his weakened body. He died in Constantinople, the first to suffer for the Faith of the Báb and the first to lay down his life for Him.

CHAPTER 9

MULLÁ ḤUSAYN UNDERTAKES A SPECIAL MISSION TO ṬIHRÁN

'Grieve not', the Báb said to Mullá Ḥusayn, 'that you have not been chosen to accompany Me on My pilgrimage to Ḥijáz. I shall, instead, direct your steps to that city which enshrines a Mystery of such transcendent holiness as neither Ḥijáz nor Shíráz can hope to rival . . . Visit, on your way, Iṣfáhán, Káshán, Ṭihrán, and Khurásán. Proceed thence to 'Iráq, and there await the summons of your Lord, who will keep watch over you and will direct you to whatsoever is His will and desire . . . The hosts of the invisible Kingdom, be assured, will sustain and reinforce your efforts. The essence of power is now dwelling in you, and the company of His chosen angels revolves around you. His almighty arms will surround you, and His unfailing Spirit will ever continue to guide your steps.'

The Báb asked Mullá Ḥusayn to write to Him when he reached Khurásán a full report of all his activities.

'Not until I receive your letter from Khurásán', He said, 'shall I be ready to set out from this city on My pilgrimage to Ḥijáz.'

Mullá Ḥusayn went first to Iṣfáhán, the next city on his route north from Shíráz. On his arrival he learnt that one of the leading Muslim teachers, a man whom Siyyid Káẓim had asked him to meet on his previous visit, had since died. Mullá Ḥusayn spoke with this teacher's disciples who opposed him fiercely and appealed to the governor of Iṣfáhán to take action against him. The governor warned them not to make mischief.

The first to accept the Báb's message in Iṣfáhán was a sifter of wheat who could not read or write. His name was Mullá Ja'far. A few others also became followers of the Báb. Mullá Ḥusayn next went to Ká<u>sh</u>án where the first to accept the message of the Báb was a prosperous merchant named Ḥájí Mírzá Jání. He then went to Qum, where Fáṭimiy-i-Máṣúmíh, the sister of the Imám Riḍa, is buried, but in that city not one person responded to his call.

On reaching Ṭihrán, he took a humble lodging at a famous religious school. The leader of the <u>Sh</u>ay<u>kh</u>í community in Ṭihrán, a certain Mírzá Muḥammad-i-<u>Kh</u>urásání, was the director of that school. Mullá Ḥusayn told him of the declaration made by the Báb, but the director did not accept the Báb's claim and instead chided Mullá Ḥusayn in these words:

'We had cherished the hope that after the death of Siyyid Káẓim you would strive to promote the best interests of the <u>Sh</u>ay<u>kh</u>í community and would deliver it from the obscurity into which it has sunk. You seem, however, to have betrayed its cause. You have shattered our fondest expectations. If you persist in disseminating these subversive doctrines, you will eventually extinguish the remnants of the <u>Sh</u>ay<u>kh</u>ís in this city.'

Mullá Ḥusayn saw that this <u>Sh</u>ay<u>kh</u>í leader was unable to understand the significance of the Báb's message and so did not burden him any further. He left his room at the school early each morning and returned to it only at sunset. However, one of the students of Mírzá Muḥammad had overheard the whole conversation between Mullá Ḥusayn and his teacher. He was deeply affected by the words of Mullá Ḥusayn and was dismayed by the arrogance of his teacher and his contemptuous dismissal of Mullá Ḥusayn.

One night, he suddenly felt that he could no longer delay and that he must speak to Mullá Ḥusayn at once. He ventured to Mullá Ḥusayn's room at midnight and found him awake and seated by the lamp. Mullá Ḥusayn greeted his young visitor with such kindness and courtesy that tears, which the young man could not restrain, flowed from his eyes.

'I can now see', Mullá Ḥusayn told him, 'the reason why I have chosen to dwell in this place. Your teacher has contemptuously rejected this Message and despised its Author. My hope is that his pupil may, unlike his master, recognise its truth. What is your name and which city is your home?'

'My name', the young man replied, 'is Mullá Muḥammad . . . My home is Núr, in the province of Mázindarán.'

'Tell me,' asked Mullá Ḥusayn, 'is there today among the family of the late Mírzá Buzurg-i-Núrí, who was so renowned for his character, his charm, and artistic and intellectual attainments, anyone who has proved himself capable of maintaining the high traditions of that illustrious house?'

'Yea,' replied Mullá Muḥammad, 'among his sons now living one has distinguished Himself by the very traits which characterised His father. By His virtuous life, His high attainments, His loving-kindness and liberality, He has proved Himself a noble descendant of a noble father.'

'What is His occupation?' asked Mullá Ḥusayn.

'He cheers the disconsolate and feeds the hungry.'

'What of His rank and position?'

'He has none apart from befriending the poor and the stranger.'

'What is His name?'

'Ḥusayn-'Alí.'

'How does He spend His time?'

'He roams the woods and delights in the beauties of the countryside.'

'What is His age?'

'Eight and twenty.'

With every reply that he received, Mullá Ḥusayn grew more joyful.

'I presume you often meet Him?' he said.

'I frequently visit His home,' replied Mullá Muḥammad.

'Will you deliver into His hands a trust from me?'

'Most assuredly.'

Mullá Ḥusayn took out a scroll of paper, wrapped it in a cloth, gave it to Mullá Muḥammad and asked him to hand it to Mírzá Ḥusayn-'Alí at dawn the next day.

'Should He deign to answer me,' he added, 'will you be kind enough to acquaint me with His reply?'

As he reached the house early the next morning, Mullá Muḥammad saw Mírzá Músá, the brother of Mírzá Ḥusayn-'Alí, standing at the gate. He explained why he had come, was taken into the house and gave the scroll of paper wrapped in the cloth to Mírzá Músá. Mírzá Músá gave it to his brother.

Mírzá Ḥusayn-'Alí asked them both to be seated while He unrolled the scroll and glanced at its contents. Then He began to read certain passages aloud. Mullá Muḥammad was much struck by the beauty of the voice he heard and by the sweetness of the verses. After He had read one page Mírzá Ḥusayn-'Alí turned to His brother and said:

'Músá, what have you to say? Verily I say, whoso believes in the Qur'án and recognises its Divine origin, and yet hesitates, though it be for a moment, to admit that these soul-stirring words are endowed with the same regenerating power, has most assuredly erred in his judgement and has strayed far from the path of justice.'

He said no more but gave Mullá Muḥammad gifts to take to Mullá Ḥusayn, some sugar and a packet of tea. He asked him to convey to Mullá Ḥusayn His loving greetings. Mullá Muḥammad hurried back. When he entered the room Mullá Ḥusayn started to his feet, received the gifts with bowed head and kissed them. Then he embraced Mullá Muḥammad, kissed his eyes and said:

'My dearly beloved friend! I pray that even as you have rejoiced my heart, God may grant you eternal felicity and fill your heart with imperishable gladness.'

Mullá Muḥammad was amazed at the behaviour of Mullá Ḥusayn and could not unravel the mystery. A few days later Mullá Ḥusayn said farewell to Mullá Muḥammad, instructing him:

'Breathe not to anyone what you have heard and witnessed. Let this be a secret hidden within your breast. Divulge not His name, for they who envy His position will arise to harm Him. In your moments of meditation, pray that the Almighty may protect Him, that, through Him, He may exalt the downtrodden, enrich the poor, and redeem the fallen. The secret of things is concealed from our eyes. Ours is the duty to raise the call of the New Day and to proclaim this Divine Message unto all people. Many a soul will, in this city, shed his blood in this path. That blood will water the Tree of God, will cause it to flourish and to overshadow all mankind.'

It was in late July 1844, about three months after the Báb declared His mission, that Mírzá Ḥusayn-'Alí accepted His message. Four years later He adopted the title 'Bahá'u'lláh' by which He is now known. This title means 'The Glory of God' and was first mentioned by the Báb in His most important book, the Bayán.

Mullá Ḥusayn left Ṭihrán through the eastern gate and took the road to Mas͟hhad and K͟hurásán praying that he might be worthy to sow the first seeds of the new Faith in that immense province.

III

Pilgrimage and Seizure

September 1844 – July 1845

CHAPTER 10

'I AM THAT QÁ'IM'

When Mullá Ḥusayn reached Mashhad, he wrote to the Báb recounting all that had happened since he left Shíráz. This letter, containing an account of his visit to Ṭihrán, brought great joy to the Báb, and he shared some of its contents with Quddús and explained to him the reason for His happiness.

As soon as he had heard from Mullá Ḥusayn the Báb began to make preparations for a pilgrimage to the holy shrines of Mecca and Medina in Arabia. One of the recorded traditions of Shí'ih Islám states that when the Promised One appears He will announce Himself at the Ka'bih in Mecca.

The Báb asked his uncle, Ḥájí Mírzá Siyyid 'Alí, to give His wife and His mother any assistance they might need in His own prolonged absence. Then, with Quddús and His Ethiopian servant as His only companions, He travelled to Búshihr where in October 1844 they boarded a boat which was bound for Jiddah in Arabia.

The boat was crowded with pilgrims, for the year 1844 was a year of the Greatest Hajj. There is a feast day celebrated by all Muslims, called the Festival of Sacrifices; it commemorates the sacrifice which Abraham offered to make of His son. It falls on the tenth day of the last Muslim month of the year and this last month is also the month of pilgrimage, when devout Muslims from all parts of the Islamic world visit Mecca and Medina. When the Feast of Sacrifices falls on a Friday, that year's pilgrimage is known as the Pilgrimage of the Greatest Hajj. Many more pilgrims than usual travel to Mecca and Medina in such a year.

In the 1840s the sea journey from Búshihr to Jiddah was a dangerous and uncomfortable one; the distance was about four thousand kilometres and the journey took about two months. The seas were often rough, storms were frequent, water was scarce and there was very little food. The Báb and Quddús remained contented and peaceful throughout the long journey. They were absorbed in their prayers and devotions for many hours at a time and the Báb revealed many writings, commentaries and letters which Quddús wrote down. However, the rigours of the sea voyage caused the Báb to beseech God that travel over the oceans of the world might soon become easier and safer.

There were two other prominent citizens of Shíráz travelling to Jiddah on the same boat. One of them was much impressed by the character of the Báb, and later, when he heard of His claim, became a Bábí; the other became an implacable enemy. The latter, a certain shaykh, became very jealous of the respect which he saw given to the Báb during the voyage and daily grew more envious. He made himself objectionable to all the passengers on the boat, molesting and trying to quarrel with everyone, but he singled out the Báb as a particular victim of his abuse and cruelty.

The Arab captain of the boat became so exasperated by this man's behaviour that he ordered his sailors to throw him overboard. When the Báb heard of this, He pleaded the shaykh's cause with the captain. The captain listened but was still determined to rid himself of this troublesome passenger. When the Báb saw the sailors preparing to hurl the man into the sea, He threw Himself at the shaykh and held onto him, begging the captain to forgive him. The captain was astonished, for he knew that the Báb had suffered more than anyone else on the boat from the insolent behaviour of the shaykh. The Báb explained to the captain that this quarrelsome man was hurting himself far more than he was hurting others by his behaviour and that, therefore, they should all be tolerant and forgiving towards him.

When they arrived in Jiddah, the Báb put on the traditional clothing of the pilgrim to Mecca, a loose tunic made of two lengths of cloth in which no seams appear, and set out across the desert to Mecca on a camel. Despite the Báb's wish that he also ride, Quddús chose to accompany Him on foot and he walked all the way from Jiddah to Mecca, a distance of about a hundred kilometres (over sixty miles), with the bridle of the Báb's camel in his hand. With a heart full of great joy, Quddús chanted many prayers as they travelled and at night he did not sleep but watched over his beloved Master.

One day the travellers stopped near a well to say their morning prayers. The Báb had left His saddlebag containing His writings and papers on the ground nearby. While they were saying their prayers a Bedouin Arab suddenly appeared, snatched up the bag and ran off with it into the desert. The Báb's servant started to run after the thief. The Báb, without interrupting His prayers, made a sign with His hand for His servant to abandon the chase. Afterwards, He explained to him kindly:

'Had I allowed you, you would surely have overtaken and punished him. But this was not to be. The papers and writings which that bag contained are destined to reach, through the instrumentality of this Arab, such places as we could never have succeeded in attaining. Grieve not, therefore, at his action, for this was decreed by God, the Ordainer, the Almighty.'

Mecca, the holy city, lies in a dip in the barren Sirat mountains. Hardly any rain falls in that area, there is scarcely any vegetation and it is very hot. Once they reached Mecca, the Báb carefully carried out all the rites of pilgrimage. On the tenth day of His pilgrimage He purchased nineteen lambs of the choicest breed and sacrificed nine in His own name, seven in the name of Quddús and three in the name of His servant. He distributed the meat amongst the poor and needy of Mecca and did not eat any of it Himself.

It was extremely hot in Mecca that year. The other pilgrims wore only their pilgrim clothing, the light and loose-fitting tunics, but the Báb, as a sign of respect for the Prophet and the shrines, did not discard His turban or cloak. With simplicity but with dignity and reverence, He circled the Ka'bih and carried out all the prescribed rites. Then, when all was completed, at a time when there was a great crowd of pilgrims present, the Báb stood against the Ka'bih, took hold of the ring on its door and called out clearly three times:

'I am that Qá'im whose advent you have been awaiting.'

A sudden hush fell upon the crowd. Many who heard those stirring words on that day took to their homes the news of the claim of the Báb, and some who heard of the incident from these pilgrims immediately accepted His message.

The Báb then wrote a letter to the sherif of Mecca, the chief religious figure in the city. In it He set out His message and called upon the sherif to accept it. Quddús delivered the letter but the sherif was very busy and did not bother to read it. A few days later Quddús inquired whether the sherif had yet read it, but he had not.

While in Mecca, the Báb met with Mírzá Muḥíṭ-i-Kirmání, a follower of Shaykh Aḥmad and Siyyid Káẓim, who had become a leading figure in the Shaykhí movement. The Báb challenged Mírzá Muḥíṭ either to accept or deny His call, but, after promising to give a reply, Mírzá Muḥíṭ went away and never gave any answer.

From Mecca the Báb went to Medina and there prayed in the holy shrine of the Prophet Muḥammad. Not far from where He prayed was the grave of Shaykh Aḥmad, that first bright star of guidance who had signalled His coming.

While on this pilgrimage, the Báb wrote to His wife: 'My sweet love . . . God is my witness that since the time of separation sorrow has been so intense that it cannot be described.' From Medina he returned to Jiddah and took ship for Persia. He arrived back at Búshihr in the early summer of 1845.

Some of the Báb's relatives and friends came to Búshihr to meet Him on His return from Mecca, for He had been away from Persia for almost nine months. While in Búshihr the Báb called Quddús to Him and asked him to travel to Shíráz ahead of Him.

'The days of your companionship with Me', the Báb told Quddús, 'are drawing to a close. The hour of separation has struck, a separation which no reunion will follow except in the Kingdom of God, in the presence of the King of Glory . . . The hand of destiny will ere long plunge you into an ocean of tribulation for His sake. I, too, will follow you; I, too, will be immersed beneath its depths. Rejoice with exceeding gladness . . .'

The Báb gave Quddús a letter to take to His uncle, Ḥájí Mírzá Siyyid 'Alí, instructed Quddús to give His loving greetings to His relatives in Shíráz and also gave him a treatise in which He listed certain devotional obligations which those who believed in Him were to carry out. He then said a loving farewell to Quddús and directed him to leave immediately for Shíráz.

CHAPTER 11
A TUMULT IN SHÍRÁZ

When Quddús reached Shíráz, Ḥájí Mírzá Siyyid 'Alí received him with great kindness and enquired eagerly after his beloved nephew. Quddús found him so receptive to the message that he explained to him the Báb's mission. Ḥájí Mírzá Siyyid 'Alí accepted the message of the Báb at once and from that time on devoted his life to the service of His cause.

The next person whom Quddús taught was a Muslim divine called Mullá Ṣádiq who became so enraptured by the treatise written by the Báb in Búshihr that he determined to carry out all the Báb's instructions at once. One of the directions of the Báb to the believers was that they should include in the traditional Islamic call to prayer some additional words which stated emphatically that 'Alí-Muḥammad (the Báb) was the servant of the Remnant of God. This title 'Remnant of God' appears in the Qur'án and was understood by Shí'ih Muslims to be an allusion to the Messenger of God they awaited.

Mullá Ṣádiq had been a famous and popular preacher and was well known for his sermons extolling the virtues of the Imáms of Islám. As he led the congregation in prayer at the mosque, he suddenly proclaimed, as he was sounding the call to prayer, the additional words prescribed by the Báb. The entire congregation broke into uproar and the learned divines, who were at the front of the congregation, raised a loud clamour of protest. 'Down with this infamous traitor! . . .' they shouted. 'Arrest him, for he is a disgrace to our

Faith.' The people behind them joined in their cries and the whole city of Shíráz was thrown into turmoil and disorder as a result of Mullá Ṣádiq's action.

The province of Fárs had been in a state of unrest and turbulence for many years and the people had repeatedly rebelled against the authority of the governors sent by the central government in Ṭihrán to rule over them. Some years earlier a group of powerful citizens, aided by the mob, had even thrown out the Sháh's own favoured brother, when he was appointed governor of Fárs province. During the latter part of 1844, while the Báb was absent from Shíráz on His pilgrimage to Mecca, the situation degenerated into anarchy. The inhabitants of the different quarters of the city feuded and fought with each other. At night so many guns were fired that no one could sleep and, in any case, people stayed awake in order to guard their homes from robbers. People were stripped naked and robbed in the main streets in broad daylight and anyone who resisted his attackers was repeatedly stabbed.

At the end of 1844 Ḥusayn Khán, a stern and uncompromising man, was posted as governor of Fárs. He arrived in Fárs in the early months of 1845 and set about restoring order at once, torturing and executing those who disturbed the public order. Soon after his arrival the city was set in uproar by Mullá Ṣádiq's unorthodox call to prayer and Ḥusayn Khán quickly enquired into the cause of the commotion. The quarrelsome shaykh whose life the Báb had saved on the voyage to Jiddah had already written to his fellow divines in Shíráz in order to arouse their fury against the Báb. Now the divines of the city united to demand that the governor punish the Báb's followers very severely.

Ḥusayn Khán ordered the arrest of Quddús, Mullá Ṣádiq and another believer, Mullá 'Alí-Akbar. The police brought them handcuffed into the presence of the governor and they also brought to Ḥusayn Khán the copy of the Báb's treatise which Mullá Ṣádiq had been reading aloud to an excited congregation at the moment of his arrest. Ḥusayn Khán looked at it and, ignoring the youthful Quddús, directed his attention to the dignified older man, Mullá Ṣádiq.

'Tell me', the governor asked angrily, as he held the treatise of the Báb in his hand, 'if you are aware of the opening passage (of this book) wherein the Siyyid-i-Báb addresses the rulers and kings of the earth in these terms:

'"*Divest yourselves of the robe of sovereignty, for He who is the King in truth, hath been made manifest!. . .*"

'If this be true, it must necessarily apply to my sovereign, Muḥammad Sháh, of the Qájár dynasty, whom I represent as the chief magistrate of this province. Must Muḥammad Sháh, according to this behest, lay down his crown and abandon his sovereignty? Must I, too, abdicate my power and relinquish my position?'

Without hesitation, Mullá Ṣádiq replied:

'When once the truth of the Revelation announced by the Author of these words shall have been definitely established, the truth of whatsoever has fallen from His lips will likewise be vindicated. If these words be the Word of God, the abdication of Muḥammad Sháh and his like can matter but little. It can in no wise turn aside the Divine purpose, nor alter the sovereignty of the almighty and eternal King.'

Ḥusayn Khán was so angry at this answer that he swore at Mullá Ṣádiq and ordered his attendants to strip him of his garments and scourge him with a thousand lashes. He also gave orders that the beards of both Quddús and Mullá Ṣádiq be burned, their noses be pierced and cords be passed through the incisions and that by these cords they should be led through the city.

'It will be an object lesson to the people of Shíráz who will know what the penalty of heresy will be,' said the governor.

Mullá Ṣádiq, calm and resigned, was heard to be reciting this prayer:

'O Lord, our God! We have indeed heard the voice of One that called. He called us to the Faith . . . and we have believed. O God, our God! Forgive us, then, our sins, and hide away from us our evil deeds, and cause us to die with the righteous.'

The savage punishment was speedily carried out and no-one intervened on behalf of Quddús and Mullá Ṣádiq or pleaded their cause. Mullá Ṣádiq's body was old and frail and many who watched thought that he would not survive the first fifty strokes of the lash. His persecutors took turns to beat him and each one beat until he became exhausted and until blood ran in streams from the lashes they cut into his back.

When the number of strokes had passed nine hundred, Mullá Ṣádiq's face was still as calm and serene as it had been at the start of the beating. He was smiling, holding his hand before his mouth, and he seemed to be completely indifferent to the blows that rained upon his frail and bleeding back.

When the scourging was over and when they had been led by their noses on halters through the city, they were expelled and warned, on pain of death, never to return to Shíráz. The governor pronounced that they would be crucified if they returned. As they were being thrown out of the city, one man who had watched Mullá Ṣádiq being beaten managed to get near enough to him to ask why he had held his hand before his mouth. Mullá Ṣádiq told him:

'The first seven strokes were severely painful; to the rest I seemed to have grown indifferent. I was wondering whether the strokes that followed were being actually applied to my own body. A feeling of joyous exultation had invaded my soul. I was trying to repress my feelings and to restrain my laughter. I can now realise how the almighty Deliverer is able, in the twinkling of an eye, to turn pain into ease, and sorrow into gladness. Immensely exalted is His power above and beyond the idle fancy of His mortal creatures.'

Quddús and Mullá Ṣádiq were the first to suffer on Persian soil in the Cause of the Báb. Mullá 'Alí had already met with suffering but in the neighbouring country of Iráq. Ḥusayn Khán was not satisfied that he had done enough and speedily sent a mounted escort of his own trusted guard to Búshihr with orders to arrest the Báb and to bring Him to Shíráz in chains.

CHAPTER 12

THE BÁB IS ARRESTED

The order of Ḥusayn Khán, governor of Shíráz, to arrest the Báb was quickly acted upon and the governor's soldiers rode swiftly towards Búshihr. As they crossed a lonely stretch of desert near Búshihr they met the Báb riding towards them accompanied by his Ethiopian servant. The Báb greeted the soldiers and asked them where they were going. The captain of the troop, having recognised the Báb, thought it best to conceal the truth and told the Báb that the governor had sent them to carry out a certain enquiry in that area. The Báb smiled:

'The governor has sent you to arrest Me,' he said. 'Here am I; do with Me as you please.'

The captain was startled and wondered that anyone could give himself up to the severe ordeal of arrest by government officials. He tried to ignore the Báb and to continue on his way but the Báb approached him and said:

'I know that you are seeking Me. I prefer to deliver Myself into your hands, rather than subject you and your companions to unnecessary annoyance for My sake.'

The captain was profoundly moved by the words of the Báb. He dismounted from his horse and kissed the stirrups of the Báb and said:

'O light of the eyes of the Prophet of God . . . I beseech you to escape from this place and to flee from before the face of Ḥusayn Khán . . . I pray you, betake yourself to the city of Mashhad . . .'

The captain promised that neither he nor any of his men would betray the Báb if he fled. The Báb refused. He said:

'May the Lord your God requite you for your magnanimity and noble intention. No one knows the mystery of My Cause; no one can fathom its secrets. Never will I turn My Face away from the decree of God. He alone is My sure Stronghold, My Stay and My Refuge. Until My last hour is at hand, none dare assail Me, none can frustrate the plan of the Almighty . . . Here am I; deliver Me into the hands of your master. Be not afraid, for no one will blame you.'

The captain bowed his head before the Báb and agreed to do as He asked. He gave his orders and the troop wheeled about and headed back towards Shíráz with the Báb riding ahead of the escort which should have bound him in chains. They continued to follow Him reverently all the way to Shíráz. The Báb rode into the city at the head of the column with a respectful cavalcade of soldiers behind Him and the people of Shíráz wondered at the sight. It was June of 1845 when the Báb returned from His pilgrimage.

The governor was angry when he heard how the Báb had entered Shíráz. At once, he summoned the Báb to him and, in front of a large group of the leading citizens of Shíráz, rudely scolded Him for His behaviour.

'Do you realise', said the angry governor, 'what a great mischief you have kindled? Are you aware what a disgrace you have become to the holy Faith of Islám and to the august person of our sovereign?'

The Báb replied with the following verse from the Qur'án: *'O believers, if an ungodly man comes to you with a tiding, make clear, lest you afflict a people unwittingly, and then repent of what you have done.'*

This reply made the governor furious.

'What!' he exclaimed. 'Dare you ascribe to us evil,

ignorance and folly?'

He ordered his attendant to strike the Báb in the face. The attendant carried out the order and struck with such a violent blow that the Báb's turban fell from His head.

The chief mullá of the city, who was present in the room, did not approve of the way the governor was treating the Báb. He tried to calm the fury of Ḥusayn Khán and urged that he be allowed to question the Báb himself, as directed in the Qur'án. The governor gave his consent and the chief mullá addressed a number of questions to Him. The Báb denied that He was either a representative of the promised Qá'im or the intermediary between Him and the faithful. The chief mullá pronounced himself satisfied with the Báb's answers and asked Him to make a public statement in the mosque on a Friday.

Ḥusayn Khán then asked that someone stand bail for the Báb, that is to say, he demanded that a respected citizen of Shíráz guarantee the Báb's good behaviour. Ḥájí Mírzá Siyyid 'Alí, the Báb's uncle, was present at the meeting, for the Báb's mother had urged him to hurry to the citadel and plead for his nephew as soon as she had heard what was going on. He stood up and offered to stand bail. The governor wanted him to allow no one to visit the Báb but Ḥájí Mírzá Siyyid 'Alí protested at this, explaining that as the Báb had just returned from pilgrimage, many people would want to come and see Him. The governor then agreed that the Báb should be allowed to receive visitors for three days but after that time, he commanded, He should see no one but his own immediate relatives.

Ḥájí Mírzá Siyyid 'Alí joyfully escorted the Báb to His home. There He was reunited with His wife and His mother. Many people visited Him during the first three days after His arrival, but after that the Báb spent His time quietly in His own home. He saw only His wife, His mother and His uncles. This was the last period of peace and tranquillity that the Báb was to know in His own home with His family. He was already a captive and was to be one for most of the remaining five years of His life.

IV

S_h_íráz

July 1845 – September 1846

CHAPTER 13

THE BÁB SPEAKS FROM THE PULPIT

While the Báb remained quietly at His home, reports came to Shíráz from other parts of Persia where His disciples were actively raising the call of the new day. Mullá Ḥusayn was journeying northwards from Ṭihrán through Khurásán province; Quddús had visited Yazd, Iṣfáhán, Káshán, Qum and Ṭihrán; and Mullá Ṣádiq had been beaten again, this time in Yazd. Shíráz seethed with stories and rumours about the Báb and the divines of the city began to clamour for action against Him. They demanded that He fulfil the pledge He had made to the governor to appear in the mosque on a Friday and clarify His position. What they wanted was for Him to make a public recantation of His claim.

The divines went together to the Imám-Jum'ih, the leading mullá who had tried to calm the fury of the governor when the Báb had been brought before him. The Imám-Jum'ih was a kindly man who was universally respected by the people of Shíráz. He was reluctant to treat any well-known citizen of the city with disrespect and he evaded the demands of the divines for as long as possible. Eventually their clamour grew so loud that he was unable to postpone action any longer and he sent a confidential message to Ḥájí Mírzá Siyyid 'Alí requesting him to bring his nephew to the mosque in order that He might fulfil the pledge He had given the governor.

'My hope', the Imám-Jum'ih confided to Ḥájí Mírzá Siyyid 'Alí, 'is that, by the aid of God the statements of your nephew may ease the tenseness of the situation and may lead to your tranquillity as well as to our own.'

The precise date on which the Báb appeared at the mosque is not known but several eye-witnesses have recounted that there was a tremendous throng of people present. From morning on, people pressed into the mosque until the cloisters, the courtyard and even the roofs and minarets were all crowded. The governor, the divines, the merchants and the notables of the city were all sitting at the front of the congregation, near to the pulpit.

About three hours before sunset, voices were heard in the courtyard and the Báb came through the gate, accompanied by ten footmen and the chief of police. He came into the mosque and walked towards the pulpit. He wore His green turban and had a loose robe over His shoulders. His bearing was sublime and such power and dignity shone from Him that the vast gathering of people seemed as nothing in His presence. He addressed Ḥusayn Khán, the governor, and the group of divines who were seated with him.

'What is your intention in asking Me to come here?'

They replied:

'The intention is that you should ascend this pulpit and repudiate your false claim so that this commotion and unrest will subside.'

The Báb said nothing but went up the first three steps of the pulpit. One of the divines who was waiting eagerly to hear the Báb renounce His claim, called out:

'Go to the top of the pulpit so that all may see and hear you.'

The Báb climbed to the top of the pulpit and sat down there. Suddenly there was complete silence in the mosque, it was so silent that it might have been quite empty of people. All who were present strained forward to hear the Báb speak. He began to give, with the utmost eloquence, majesty and power, an address in Arabic on the subject of Divine Unity.

For about half an hour high and low, learned and illiterate, listened attentively, in complete silence. Then the shaykh who had called out to the Báb to climb to the top of the pulpit turned furiously to the governor and said:

'Did you bring this Siyyid here, into the presence of all these people, to prove His Cause, or did you bring Him to recant and renounce His false claim? He will soon with these words win over all these people to His side. Tell Him to say what He has to say. What are all these idle tales?'

The governor then addressed the Báb:

'O Siyyid! say what you have been told to say. What is this idle chatter?'

The Báb was silent for a moment and then he spoke to all who were gathered there:

'O people!' He said, 'Know this well that I speak what My Grandfather, the Messenger of God, spoke twelve hundred and sixty years ago, and I do not speak what My Grandfather did not.'

He then quoted a well-known Muslim tradition:

'*What Muḥammad made lawful remains lawful unto the Day of Resurrection and what He forbade remains forbidden unto the Day of Resurrection.*'

He went on, quoting another tradition from the Imáms:

'*Whenever the Qá'im arises that will be the Day of Resurrection.*'

Having spoken these words, the Báb descended from the pulpit. When He came face to face with the shaykh who had chided the governor a few minutes earlier, the infuriated divine raised his walking-stick and struck at the Báb but a young man of the city, seeing what was about to happen, stepped forward and took the blow that was intended for the Báb on his own shoulder. The Báb intended to join the congregation in the observance of prayer but the Imám-Jum'ih, fearing that He might be attacked and injured as the crowd dispersed from the mosque, requested Him to return home at once.

'Your family', he said, 'is anxiously awaiting your return. All are apprehensive lest any harm befall you. Repair to your house and there offer your prayer; of greater merit shall this deed be in the sight of God.'

The Báb went straight home. He had succeeded in calming the people as the governor had requested. His claim was not false and could not therefore be renounced, but He had, by implication, announced for all who had ears to hear Him, that He was a Messenger of God. Those amongst the congregation who were already His followers were strengthened in their faith for they perceived that the Báb had publicly affirmed His claim. Others who saw and heard Him on that day became His followers. The news of His appearance and His statement from the pulpit quickly spread beyond Shíráz.

The demand of the divines that He appear at the mosque had achieved exactly the opposite of what they had intended and they became extremely angry. As soon as they could meet together, they passed a sentence of death on the Báb.

The divines had invited the Imám-Jum'ih to attend their meeting but he had refused, knowing well what they intended to do. After the meeting, the divines took to him a paper pronouncing sentence of death on the Báb and asked him to put his seal of approval on it. The Imám-Jum'ih read the paper and dashed it to the ground angrily.

'Have you gone out of your minds?' he said and went on, 'I will never put my seal on this paper, because I have no doubts about the lineage, integrity, piety, nobility and honesty of this Siyyid. I see that this young Man is possessed of all the virtues of Islám and humanity and of all the faculties of intellect . . . Away with you and your false imaginings, away, away!'

After his appearance at the mosque, the Báb was able to

spend some time peacefully with His family and He celebrated Naw-Rúz of 1845, the first Naw-Rúz since He had declared His mission, quietly in His own home.

The Báb had originally intended to travel back to Shíráz from Mecca by way of Karbilá and there were a few Bábís in Karbilá who were anxiously waiting for Him to arrive there. Soon after Naw-Rúz of 1845 these Bábís received a letter from the Báb informing them that He had altered His plans and was already back in Shíráz. In this letter He directed them to go to Iṣfáhán and wait there for further instructions.

'Should it be deemed advisable,' He had written to them, 'We shall request you to proceed to Shíráz; if not, tarry in Iṣfáhán until such time as God may make known to you His will and guidance.'

This letter agitated the minds and tested the loyalty of the Bábís in Karbilá. 'What of His promise to us?' a few discontented believers whispered. 'Does He regard the breaking of His pledge as the interposition of the will of God?' However, most of the believers in Karbilá accepted the directions of the Báb and clung with added fervour to His Cause. They set off joyfully towards Iṣfáhán and at the town of Kangavar they met Mullá Ḥusayn who, with his brother and nephew, was making his way to Karbilá, as instructed by the Báb.

When Mullá Ḥusayn heard that the Báb was under house arrest in Shíráz, he decided to make for Iṣfáhán with the others. On that journey he was so overjoyed at the thought of being near to the Báb once again that he enkindled the hearts of all his companions. They were lost in admiration for the brilliant qualities of his mind and heart and were greatly stirred by his example. As they neared Iṣfáhán, Mullá Ḥusayn advised them to enter the city in small groups so as not to attract attention, and his advice was followed.

A few days after their arrival in Iṣfáhán, news of the Báb reached them. They heard that no one was allowed to see

Him and they learnt that it would be very dangerous for them to try to enter Shíráz. Mullá Ḥusayn was quite undeterred by this news and determined to go on. He disguised himself as a tribesman, rode on horseback to Shíráz and stopped a little outside the city to wait for darkness. In the quiet of the night he sent his brother to the house of Ḥájí Mírzá Siyyid 'Alí.

The next day, soon after sunset, Ḥájí Mírzá Siyyid 'Alí came out of the city and cautiously escorted Mullá Ḥusayn to the safety of his own house. The Báb came to His uncle's house at night several times and remained there till dawn in the company of his beloved first disciple. The Bábís who were waiting in Iṣfáhán were summoned, one by one, to enter the city secretly. They came and they too attained the presence of the Báb.

Despite the care which Mullá Ḥusayn had taken with his disguise, he was recognised and his enemies denounced him to the authorities, so that it became impossible for him to remain in the city.

The Báb directed him to go to Yazd and from Yazd to travel to Khurásán province. He sent all the other Bábís, except one who acted as His secretary, back to Iṣfáhán. As they moved away from Shíráz, a new wave of teaching began which was soon to be felt in every corner of the country. Once again, those who had denounced the Bábís had achieved exactly the opposite of what they had intended, for as the Bábís spread out from Shíráz, news of the Báb spread with them through every section of society from the humblest village to the royal court of the Sháh.

CHAPTER 14

PERSIA IN DISTRESS

In 1845, while the Báb was under house arrest, the ruler of Persia was Muḥammad S͟háh, a grandson of Fatḥ-'Alí S͟háh, whose long reign had ended in 1834.

The S͟háh of Persia was not bound by any written constitution but had absolute power over his subjects. The Persian state was formally religious but the early strength and purity of Islamic society had long disappeared. The S͟háh was surrounded by courtiers who acted as advisers, but he could not rely on the accuracy of the information given to him by these courtiers. The administration of the country was corrupt from the highest to the lowest level and everyone gave and received bribes. There was no court of law which could be relied upon to execute justice, but the courts were, instead, notorious for the savage punishments they inflicted on those who were brought before them. A few people in Persia lived in great wealth while the mass of the population lived in poverty and ignorance.

Fatḥ-'Alí S͟háh had proved himself to be a weak-minded and incompetent ruler. Encouraged by the British, he had undertaken a series of wars against Russia which were disastrous for Persia and which had led to the humiliating defeat of the Persian army in 1828. During the reign of Fatḥ-'Alí S͟háh, two men had stood out from their contemporaries. One had been the heir to the throne, Crown Prince 'Abbás Mírzá. The other was his advisor, a man called Mírzá Abu'l Qásim, Qá'im-Maqám-i-Faráhání. These two men had tried hard to improve the condition of their country. The Crown

Prince had opposed the policy of war with Russia and had sought to improve the Persian army by reshaping it along European lines. The strength of the Persian army had, however, always lain in the swift mobility of its mounted tribesmen and the efforts of the Crown Prince to drill the Persian soldiers in European ways had only weakened the army in the field. The Crown Prince had also proved to be a disastrously incompetent leader in battle, and for his own personal advantage had given away several disputed territories to Russia. The pressures of military defeat and of factional fighting and intrigue at his father's court had proved too much for him and he died in 1833 at the age of forty-five, a sad and broken man. Despite his faults, his premature death was a loss to Persia. A year later, his father, Fatḥ-'Alí Sháh, died leaving a family of fifty-three sons and forty-six daughters.

In the 1830s Persia was so enfeebled a country that other powers were easily able to interfere in her internal affairs. Before his death, Crown Prince 'Abbás Mírzá had obtained the support of the Russian government for his own eldest son's succession to the throne. This son, Muḥammad Sháh, succeeded to the throne with the support of both Russia and Britain and as a result of the wise strategy of his father's faithful minister, Qá'im-Maqám. In the first year of his rule, Muḥammad Sháh arranged for Qá'im-Maqám to be murdered. In his death Persia lost an honest minister and a brilliant statesman. Because the sháhs were surrounded by many advisors whom they could not trust, they chose to rely on the advice of one favoured courtier who was given the title of Grand Vizier. Having disposed of Qá'im-Maqám, Muḥammad Sháh took as his Grand Vizier a man named Ḥájí Mírzá Áqásí, his former tutor and religious instructor.

A British diplomat, Sir Henry Layard, had an audience with Ḥájí Mírzá Áqásí in 1840. This is how he wrote of him:

'We waited upon the Prime Minister, the Ḥájí Mírzá Áqásí, who was then the man of the greatest influence, power and authority in Persia. The Sháh had committed to him almost the entire government of his kingdom, occupying himself but little with public affairs, aware of his own incapacity for conducting them.

'The Ḥájí . . . was, by all accounts, a statesman of craft and cunning, but of limited abilities. He was cruel and treacherous, proud and overbearing, although he affected the humility of a pious mulla . . . The religious character which he had assumed made him intolerant and bigoted, and he was known to be a fanatical hater of Christians . . . His misgovernment, and the corruption and general oppression which everywhere existed had brought Persia to the verge of ruin. Distress, misery, and discontent prevailed to an extent previously unknown . . . He was a man of small stature, with sharp and somewhat mean and forbidding features and a loud, shrill voice.'

As the rumours of the young Siyyid of Shíráz rippled through the royal court, the Sháh decided to send someone to investigate the matter. He chose as his envoy a man named Siyyid Yaḥyáy-i-Dárábí. The Sháh chose him because he was famous throughout Persia as a learned, eloquent and influential religious teacher. Other religious leaders had often testified to his mature wisdom, his unparalleled knowledge and his excellent judgement, for when Siyyid Yaḥyá was present at a meeting he was automatically its chief speaker and all were silent and reverent before him. The Sháh had complete faith in his judgement.

At this time, Siyyid Yaḥyá was staying in Ṭihrán as a guest of the Sháh at the home of one of the leading courtiers of the royal household. The Sháh instructed that the following message be delivered to him:

'Tell him from us that inasmuch as we repose the utmost

confidence in his integrity, and admire his moral and intellectual standards, and regard him as the most suitable among the divines of our realm, we expect him to proceed to Shíráz, to enquire thoroughly into the episode of the Siyyid-i-Báb, and to inform us of the results of his investigations. We shall then know what measures it behoves us to take.'

CHAPTER 15

THE SHÁH'S ENVOY

Siyyid Yaḥyá had wanted to go to Shíráz to enquire into the Cause of the Báb, but circumstances had so far prevented him from doing so. He now travelled in state as the Sháh's trusted envoy and was received with honour in Shíráz by the city's governor, Ḥusayn Khán. On his journey he had turned the matter over in his mind, had decided that he could easily overcome the Báb in argument and had resolved on all the questions he would put to him. He thought that he would quickly give his verdict on the Cause of the Báb and then return to Ṭihrán where he would deal with more important matters.

Siyyid Yaḥyá stayed in Shíráz as the governor's personal guest, and arrangements were made for him to meet the Báb at the house of Ḥájí Mírzá Siyyid 'Alí. Siyyid Yaḥyá greeted the Báb courteously and then for two hours asked Him questions on the most difficult and obscure points in Islamic teaching. The Báb listened calmly to all that Siyyid Yaḥyá said and noted all his questions. When Siyyid Yaḥyá finished speaking, the Báb replied. Siyyid Yaḥyá marvelled at the brief, clear answers that the Báb gave him. He was overcome by a feeling of shame and he sensed his own utter lowliness. He, who for so long had been the centre of attention in any gathering, felt now, in the presence of the Báb, only his own presumption and pride. He brought the interview to a close with these words:

'Please God, I shall, in the course of my next audience with You, submit the rest of my questions and with them shall conclude my enquiry.'

Before his second interview with the Báb, Siyyid Yaḥyá again prepared a list of questions that he wished to ask. But when he came into the presence of the Báb, he found that all these questions were vanishing from his mind. He was bewildered and asked only a few questions which he knew were not even relevant to the enquiry. He was then even more bewildered to hear the Báb answering, with that same brevity and clarity, those same questions that he had been unable to ask. Yet he doubted what he heard and saw. He was so confused, so upset and bewildered by what had happened that he could not think clearly. He asked for leave to retire.

Once he was out of the presence of the Báb, Siyyid Yaḥyá resolved that in his next interview he would test the Báb. He would ask the Báb just one question, not outwardly, but in his heart. He would silently request the Báb to reveal a commentary on the Súrih of Kaw<u>th</u>ar. He resolved that if the Báb granted his unspoken wish and revealed this commentary, he would at once acknowledge His claim and accept His teachings. If He did not, Siyyid Yaḥyá would reject His claim.

As soon as he was again in the presence of the Báb, Siyyid Yaḥyá was seized with a great fear. He could not understand this. He had been so many times in the presence of the <u>Sh</u>áh but had never felt a single trace of timidity. Now, in the presence of the Báb, he was so awed and shaken that he could not even stand upright but swayed on his feet. The Báb saw his condition and rose from His seat. He came towards Siyyid Yaḥyá, took him gently by the hand and led him to sit beside Him.

'Seek from Me', said the Báb, 'whatever is your heart's desire. I will readily reveal it to you.'

Siyyid Yaḥyá could not reply. He felt like an infant who could neither speak nor understand what was spoken. The

Báb smiled at him and said:

'Were I to reveal for you the commentary on the Súrih of Kawthar, would you acknowledge that My words are born of the Spirit of God? Would you recognise that My utterance can in no wise be associated with sorcery or magic?'

As he heard these words, Siyyid Yaḥyá began to weep and all that he could manage to say was this verse from the Qur'án:

'O our Lord, with ourselves have we dealt unjustly; if Thou forgive us not and have not pity on us, we shall surely be of those who perish.'

The Báb then asked His uncle to bring His pen-case and some paper. Siyyid Yaḥyá has left a vivid account of what followed as the Báb began to reveal the commentary on the Súrih of Kawthar:

'How am I to describe this scene of inexpressible majesty? Verses streamed from His pen with a rapidity that was truly astounding. The incredible swiftness of His writing, the soft and gentle murmur of His voice, and the stupendous force of His style, amazed and bewildered me. He continued in this manner until the approach of sunset. He did not pause until the entire commentary of the Súrih was completed. He then laid down His pen and asked for tea. Soon after, He began to read it aloud in my presence. My heart leaped madly as I heard Him pour out, in accents of unutterable sweetness, those treasures enshrined in that sublime commentary. I was so entranced by its beauty that three times over I was on the verge of fainting. He sought to revive my failing strength with a few drops of rose-water which He caused to be sprinkled on my face. This restored my vigour and enabled me to follow His reading to the end.'

Siyyid Yaḥyá stayed at the house of Ḥájí Mírzá Siyyid 'Alí for three nights while he and one other Bábí copied out the Báb's commentary and checked all the traditions quoted in it against the Islamic texts. There was not a single error. Siyyid Yaḥyá was utterly convinced of the truth of the Báb's mission. He wrote later:

'Such was the state of certitude to which I had attained that if all the powers of the earth were to be leagued against me they would be powerless to shake my confidence in the greatness of His Cause.'

Ḥusayn Khán was angry and suspicious that Siyyid Yaḥyá had stayed away from him so long. He enquired what he was doing and whether he had fallen victim to the Báb's magic influence. Siyyid Yaḥyá sent this reply:

'No one but God, who alone can change the hearts of men, is able to captivate the heart of Siyyid Yaḥyá. Whoso can ensnare his heart is of God, and His word unquestionably the voice of Truth.'

Ḥusayn Khán was alarmed. He wrote to the Sháh complaining bitterly of his guest's behaviour, for Siyyid Yaḥyá had refused to meet with the 'ulamás, the learned men of the city. The Sháh sent this reply:

'It is strictly forbidden to any one of our subjects to utter such words as would tend to detract from the exalted rank of Siyyid Yaḥyáy-i-Dárábí. He is of noble lineage, a man of great learning, of perfect and consummate virtue. He will under no circumstances incline his ear to any cause unless he believes it to be conducive to the advancement of the best interests of our realm and to the well-being of the Faith of Islám.'

It was also reported that Muḥammad Sháh spoke the following words to his Grand Vizier, Ḥájí Mírzá Áqásí, at this time.

'We have been lately informed that Siyyid Yaḥyáy-i-Dárábí has become a Bábí. If this be true, it behoves us to cease belittling the cause of that siyyid.'

Siyyid Yaḥyá wrote a report to the Sháh and sent it to him

but he did not return to the capital.

The Báb gave the name 'Vahíd', meaning the Unique or Peerless One, to Siyyid Yaḥyá. He directed Vahíd to first visit his father in Luristán and then to begin teaching. Vahíd's father, while not rejecting the message of the Báb outright, showed no wish to be identified with this new movement and Vahíd did not burden him further. He began to travel and in every town that he visited, he spread the good news of the coming of the Báb from the pulpits of the mosques until the whole country was astir with the story. Most of the other religious teachers declared that the revered and erudite Siyyid Yaḥyá had either gone mad or been bewitched.

News of Vahíd's activities reached the town of Zanján, to the west of Ṭihrán, where there lived a religious teacher and leader called Mullá Muḥammad-'Alí. He was an extremely forceful and outspoken character, enormously knowledgeable and a fluent and lucid speaker. He was an independent-minded individual and always said exactly what he thought, regardless of the consequences, and he often upset the other religious teachers by expressing his own ideas so forcefully. He criticised the actions of the Shí'ite clergy and often expressed his horror at what they had done in the past. On several occasions the Sháh had intervened in these disputes in order to save Mullá Muḥammad-'Alí from the wrath of his fellow divines and to prevent grave disorder and bloodshed in Zanján.

When he heard that Siyyid Yaḥyá had become a Bábí, Mullá Muḥammad-'Alí sent a trusted messenger to Shíráz to find out more about the Báb. His messenger returned at a time when all the divines of the city of Zanján were gathered with Mullá Muḥammad-'Alí. He asked his envoy if he had himself accepted the message of the Báb and the man replied that he would follow the decision of his master. On hearing this, Mullá Muḥammad-'Alí grew very angry.

'How dare you', he cried, 'consider matters of belief to be dependent upon the approbation or rejection of others?'

He took a copy of the Báb's writing which the messenger had brought from Shíráz and began to read it. When he had read only one page, he fell on his face as if in prayer and cried out to the assembled company:

'I bear witness that these words which I have read proceed from the same Source as that of the Qur'án. Whoso has recognised the truth of that sacred Book must needs testify to the Divine origin of these words, and must needs submit to the precepts inculcated by their Author. I take you, members of this assembly, as my witnesses; I pledge such allegiance to the Author of this Revelation that should He ever pronounce the night to be the day, and declare the sun to be a shadow, I would unreservedly submit to His judgement, and would regard His verdict as the voice of Truth.'

The Báb gave the name of Ḥujjat to Mullá Muḥammad-'Alí. It means the Proof. Ḥujjat, like Vahíd, at once began to travel and spread the teachings of the Báb.

CHAPTER 16

FAREWELL TO SHÍRÁZ

The Báb celebrated the second Naw-Rúz after the declaration of His mission, in the spring of 1846, still under house arrest, but in circumstances of comparative ease and tranquillity. He showed great love to both His wife and His mother, cheered their hearts with His tender affection and dispelled their fears for His future.

In the early summer of 1846, when He had been back in Shíráz for almost a year, the Báb wrote His will, bequeathing all His property jointly to His mother and His wife. Amongst His relatives, only His wife and His uncle believed in His mission at this stage. The Báb shared with His wife the secret of His future sufferings and explained to her the significance of what would happen to Him, thus giving her strength and courage to bear what was to come. He asked her not to share this knowledge with His mother but to be patient and resigned to the will of God. He gave her a special prayer which He assured her would remove her difficulties and lighten her sorrow. This is the prayer:

'*Is there any Remover of difficulties save God? Say: Praised be God! He is God! All are His servants and all abide by His bidding!*'

'In the hour of your perplexity', the Báb told her, 'recite this prayer ere you go to sleep. I Myself will appear to you and will banish your anxiety.'

The Báb knew how soon He would have to leave them but in the few months that He remained with His family, He continued to cheer their hearts and dispel their fears. He moved to His uncle's house and told the few Bábís who had settled in Shíráz to go to Iṣfáhán and wait there for His instructions.

The divines in Shíráz were still clamouring for action against the Báb and Ḥusayn Khán, the governor, was jealous of the considerable influence that the Báb exerted in the city, even under house arrest. The governor kept a continual watch on the Báb through his spies and tried hard to degrade Him in the eyes of the public.

The Grand Vizier, too, had his spies and kept a close watch on Shíráz. He jealously guarded his own position of influence over the Sháh and was alert to anything that might weaken it. Ḥusayn Khán knew that the Grand Vizier would be very happy to learn that the Bábí movement had ceased to exist and that its Founder had perished.

One night, the governor's chief spy came to him with a most alarming report. He told the governor that the number of people crowding to see the Báb was so great that the governor should take immediate action before the security of the city was further imperilled.

'The eager crowd that gathers every night to visit the Báb', he said, 'surpasses in number the multitude of people that throngs every day before the gates of the seat of your government . . . If you would permit me, I will, with the aid of a number of your attendants, surprise the Báb at the hour of midnight and will deliver, handcuffed, into your hands certain of his associates who will enlighten you concerning his activities, and who will confirm the truth of my statements.'

Ḥusayn Khán did not agree to this plan.

'I can tell better than you', he answered, 'what the interests of the State require. Watch me from a distance; I shall know how to deal with him.'

At once the governor summoned to him the chief constable of the city.

'Proceed immediately', he ordered him, 'to the house of Ḥájí Mírzá Siyyid 'Alí. Quietly and unobserved, scale the wall and ascend to the roof, and from there suddenly enter his home. Arrest the Siyyid-i-Báb immediately, and conduct him to this place together with any of the visitors who may be present with him at that time. Confiscate whatever books and documents you are able to find in that house . . . I swear by the imperial diadem of Muḥammad Sháh that this very night I shall have the Siyyid-i-Báb executed together with his wretched companions. Their ignominious death will quench the flame they have kindled, and will awaken every would-be follower of that creed to the danger that awaits every disturber of the peace of this realm. By this act I shall have extirpated a heresy the continuance of which constitutes the gravest menace to the interests of the State.'

The chief constable hurried away to carry out the governor's orders. He and his men climbed the walls of the house and entered it from the roof. They found the Báb with His uncle and one other Bábí. The constable told all three that they were under arrest, collected together all the papers that he could find in the house and ordered Ḥájí Mírzá Siyyid 'Alí to remain in his house. He led the Báb and His companion away. The Báb was serene and composed. He was heard reciting a verse of the Qur'án:

'*That with which they are threatened is for the morning. Is not the morning near?*'

The constable led the Báb and His companion through the dark streets. As they reached the city market-place, the constable saw with horror a long procession of coffins being carried through the streets by a crowd of weeping and wailing citizens. An exceptionally sudden and fierce outbreak of cholera had occurred and in the few hours since midnight the dreaded disease had killed over one hundred people. There was no treatment or cure for cholera at that time and no one knew how the disease spread or how to prevent it. An outbreak of cholera was the signal for mass panic in any part of the country. Everyone would flee in terror, abandoning any members of their family who showed symptoms of the disease.

The constable, overcome with fear, ran to the house of the governor. The large house was deserted. An elderly watchman told him that three of the servants were already dead and that a number of the family were dangerously ill. The governor had fled with the rest of his family out of the city.

Very shaken by this news, the constable decided to take the Báb to his own home. As they reached his house, they heard fresh cries of agony and pain. The constable's son was near death. The distraught father threw himself at the feet of the Báb and begged him to save the boy's life.

'Suffer not that he, in the prime of youth, be taken away from me,' he implored. 'Punish him not for the guilt which his father has committed. I repent of what I have done and at this moment resign my post. I solemnly pledge my word that never again will I accept such a position even though I perish of hunger.'

The Báb was about to say the prayer of dawn. He gave the constable some of the water with which He was washing His face and told him to give it to his son to drink. The constable quickly obeyed and the boy began to recover. The grateful man wrote at once to the governor:

'Have pity on yourself as well as on those whom Providence has committed to your care. Should the fury of this plague continue its fatal course, no one in this city, I fear, will by the end of this day have survived the horror of its attack.'

The governor replied that the Báb should immediately be released and given the freedom to go anywhere he liked as long as it was away from Shíráz.

The Báb stayed at the constable's house but sent the companion who had been arrested with Him to fetch His uncle. He told His uncle that He planned to go to Iṣfáhán, and sent with him messages of love and comfort for His wife and mother. As He said farewell to His uncle, He assured him:

'God's all-encompassing love and protection will surround them. I will again meet you amid the mountains of Ádhirbáyján . . .'

V

Iṣfáhán

October 1846 – March 1847

CHAPTER 17

THE BÁB IS MADE WELCOME IN IṢFÁHÁN

The Báb left Shíráz at the end of September 1846 and travelled north through the dry autumn land for three hundred miles to Iṣfáhán. Ḥusayn Khán was furious that he had not been able to put the Báb to death and as soon as He was out of the city, ordered that Ḥájí Mírzá Siyyid 'Alí be brought to him. He commanded that this highly respected merchant be beaten and this was done. Ḥusayn Khán then turned his attention to the Báb's brother-in-law, a man who was so seriously ill that he could not get up from his bed. Ḥusayn Khán's men broke into his house, dragged him out of bed and hauled him before the governor who cursed him, threatened him with vile punishments and made him pay a large fine.

Ḥusayn Khán then proclaimed that anyone found with a single sheet of the Báb's writing in their possession would be severely punished. Scores of people hurried to the house of the Báb's brother-in-law, tossed inside papers containing the Báb's writings and ran away before they could be seen. The Báb's uncle advised the family to wash away the ink and bury the sheets of paper.

While His relatives in Shíráz bore the brunt of the governor's anger, the Báb was approaching the outskirts of Iṣfáhán.

To any traveller crossing the dry, stony land, the first sight of Iṣfáhán is as of a mirage of lovely domes set amongst palms and fruit trees. Sháh 'Abbas, who ruled Persia in the late sixteenth and early seventeenth centuries, made Iṣfáhán the capital of his kingdom and built there many beautiful mosques, colleges and palaces and surrounded them with lovely gardens. So magnificent was Iṣfáhán in his reign that people began to call it 'Niṣf-i-Jahán', which means 'Half the World'. But in 1722 an Afghán army besieged the city and destroyed a large part of it. Hundreds of thousands of people died in and around the city of hunger and disease. More than a century later Iṣfáhán had not recovered from the devastation of the Afghán invasion and many of its fine buildings were still in ruins. However, the city was famous throughout Persia and beyond for the erudition of its divines and the fervour of its Shí'ite inhabitants.

The governor of Iṣfáhán was a man named Manúchihr Khán. He was born in Georgia in the south of Russia, had been sold into slavery as a child and was made a eunuch by his Persian owners. He was brought up as a Muslim but had never been personally convinced of the truth of Muḥammad's mission. He had been employed in the public service, had risen to the highest posts and had the reputation of being the best administrator in the kingdom.

Manúchihr Khán was also a professional soldier. He had fought many battles for the Sháh and had pacified a large area of the country for him. The Sháh had great confidence in Manúchihr Khán but many people hated and feared him because of his harsh and cruel actions. On one occasion, after putting down a rebellion, he had made a tower out of the living bodies of seventy or more of the prisoners he had taken. Despite such acts, Manúchihr Khán was generally agreed to be a just governor. He protected the weak from the oppression of the strong and under his governorship life was more secure than in many other parts of Persia. He had been given the post of governor of the great province of Iṣfáhán as a reward for his services to the Sháh.

While nearing the city, the Báb wrote a letter to Manúchihr Khán asking where He might stay in Iṣfáhán. This letter was phrased in such courteous terms and was written in such exquisite handwriting that it made a deep impression on the governor. He ordered the chief of the mullás of the city to go out and receive the Báb and instructed him to welcome Him as his guest in his own home. The chief mullá sent a group of his close friends out to greet the Báb and then went himself to escort the Báb to his house.

On that first night the chief mullá was so much impressed by the Báb that, disregarding his own rank and station, he seized the ewer of water from the hand of his chief steward and himself poured out the water over the hands of the Báb. From that moment onwards, he saw personally to the needs and wants of his guest. Many learned and distinguished divines began to visit the house of the chief mullá in order to see the Báb. One night, when a number of guests were present, the chief mullá asked the Báb to reveal a commentary on a certain chapter of the Qur'án. The Báb at once took pen and paper and began to write. When He had finished, He began to chant the long commentary that He had composed. The guests were astounded and overwhelmed by the power of His words. Instinctively, they started to their feet and, together with their host, the chief mullá, they knelt and kissed the hem of the Báb's robe. One of the divines who was there broke into a sudden exclamation of praise:

'Peerless and unique', he exclaimed, 'as are the words which have streamed from this pen, to be able to reveal, within so short a time and in so legible a writing, so great a number of verses as to equal a fourth, nay a third, of the Qur'án, is in itself an achievement such as no mortal, without the intervention of God, could hope to perform.'

As the Báb's fame spread throughout the city, a stream of visitors came to the house of the chief mullá from every quarter. Some were merely curious but others sought a deeper understanding of the Báb's teachings; yet others asked for remedies for their illnesses and suffering. The governor heard what was happening and decided that he too should pay a visit to the Báb.

CHAPTER 18

THE GRAND VIZIER STIRS UP TROUBLE

On the day that Manúchihr Khán went to the chief mullá's house to see the Báb, he found Him seated with a group of the most learned and famous divines of the city.

The governor had, on a number of previous occasions, requested these same people to convince him of the truth of Muḥammad's mission but not one of them had been able to give him a satisfying answer. He now made the same request to the Báb.

'Which do you prefer,' asked the Báb, 'a verbal or a written answer to your question?'

'A written reply', Manúchihr Khán answered, 'not only would please those who are present at this meeting but would edify and instruct both the present and future generations.'

At once the Báb began to write. He wrote for nearly two hours and covered fifty pages of script with a stimulating account of the origin, character and pervasive influence of Islám. His sound reasoning, the accuracy of detail and the vigour of His style removed all the doubts that had remained for so long in the mind of the governor.

'Hear me!' Manúchihr Khán exclaimed joyfully. 'Members of this revered assembly, I take you as my witnesses. Never until this day have I in my heart been firmly convinced of the truth of Islám. I can henceforth, thanks to this exposition penned by this Youth, declare myself a firm believer in the Faith proclaimed by the Apostle of God. I solemnly testify to my belief in the reality of the superhuman power with which this Youth is endowed, a power which no amount of learning can ever impart.'

As the fame of the Báb spread through the city and beyond it, a number of the divines became jealous of the respect given to Him and of the influence which He was gaining over their own followers. The Sháh's chief minister, Ḥájí Mírzá Áqásí, became seriously alarmed at the reports reaching him from Iṣfáhán. He feared that Manúchihr Khán, the trusted and faithful servant of the Sháh, would be able to arrange for the Sháh to meet the Báb. He was terrified that the impressionable and tender-hearted Sháh would be won over by the person and the teachings of the Báb and that this would bring an end to his own career.

Ḥájí Mírzá Áqásí wrote to the chief mullá of Iṣfáhán, scolding him for the deference which he had shown to the Báb:

'We have expected you', he chided, 'to resist with all your power every cause which conflicts with the best interests of the government and people of this land. You seem instead to have befriended, nay to have glorified, the author of this obscure and contemptible movement.'

He also wrote to a number of divines in the city, whom he had previously ignored, encouraging them to oppose the Báb. The chief mullá continued to maintain a respectful attitude to the Báb but he began to make it more difficult for the Báb's guests to meet Him. One of the divines in the city began to abuse the Báb from his pulpit.

When Manúchihr Khán heard what was happening, he sent a message to the chief mullá reminding him of the visit he had paid to the Báb in his home and inviting both him and the Báb to his own home. He invited the other learned divines but two of them refused to accept the invitation as they feared that they would be the losers in any debate with the Báb. When all the others were assembled, the divines began to question the Báb and He answered clearly and politely all the questions put to Him, but one of the divines was dissatisfied with an answer and began an idle argument.

When the governor saw what was happening, he quickly brought the meeting to an end and gave instructions that the chief mullá be conducted immediately to his home. He did not think that it was safe for the Báb to return to the chief mullá's home as he feared that the divines might take some violent action against Him. Manúchihr Khán offered the hospitality of his own home to the Báb. The Báb accepted and stayed there for a few weeks.

The divines of Iṣfáhán, dismayed and enraged at what had happened, met together and passed a sentence of death on the Báb. They prepared a document signed and sealed by about seventy eminent 'ulamá and notables of the city pronouncing the Báb a heretic deserving of death. Only two of the divines of Iṣfáhán refused to have their names associated with this document. The chief mullá would not endorse the death-warrant but he added an evasive reply to the paper. He wrote:

'I testify that in the course of my association with this youth I have been unable to discover any act that would in any way betray his repudiation of the doctrines of Islám. On the contrary, I have known him as a pious and loyal observer of its precepts. The extravagance of his claims, however, and his disdainful contempt for the things of the world, incline me to believe that he is devoid of reason and judgement.'

When the governor heard what the divines had done, he devised a plan to ensure the safety of the Báb. In order to calm the anxiety which had arisen in the city and prevent public disorder, he announced that the Báb had been summoned to Ṭihrán. He decided to send the Báb out of the city with an escort of five hundred horsemen. He then arranged that after they had all gone a certain distance, one hundred of these horsemen should leave the escort and return to the city. This would happen every few miles until only one hundred men would be left with the Báb. Of these, twenty at a time should return at regular intervals until only twenty of the governor's most trusted and loyal men remained. Ten of these should then be sent to another area to collect taxes for the governor and the remaining ten would bring the Báb back into Iṣfáhán in disguise along a little-used road. This small escort would bring the Báb, before daybreak, in the utmost secrecy, to the private apartments of the governor's official residence.

Thousands of the citizens of Iṣfáhán crowded to watch as the Báb left the city escorted by this large company of soldiers.

CHAPTER 19

MANÚCHIHR KHÁN SHELTERS THE BÁB

The governor's plan to hide the Báb in his own home went smoothly and before dawn of the next day He was safely back in the house. Manúchihr Khán waited on his Guest himself, served His meals and saw to His needs. No one knew where the Báb was. Wild rumours began to circulate that He had been executed in Ṭihrán or killed on the way there. In order to calm the fears of the Bábís, the Báb allowed three of the believers in Iṣfáhán to be brought to Him. He instructed the others to leave Iṣfáhán and go north to Káshán, Qum or Ṭihrán.

One day, while he was sitting in his private garden within the courtyard of his house, Manúchihr Khán confided to his Guest that he had a plan which he believed would make it possible for the Sháh to accept the new teachings. This is what he proposed:

'The almighty Giver has endowed me with great riches. I know not how best to use them. Now that I have, by the aid of God, been led to recognise this Revelation, it is my ardent desire to consecrate all my possessions to the furtherance of its interests and the spread of its fame. It is my intention to proceed, by Your leave, to Ṭihrán and to do my best to win to this Cause Muḥammad Sháh, whose confidence in me is firm and unshaken. I am certain that he will eagerly embrace it, and will arise to promote it far and wide. I will also endeavour to induce the Sháh to dismiss the profligate Ḥájí Mírzá Áqásí, the folly of whose administration has well-nigh brought this land to the verge of ruin. Next, I will strive to obtain for You the hand of one of the sisters of the Sháh, and will myself undertake the preparation of Your nuptials. Finally, I hope to be enabled to incline the hearts of the rulers and kings of the earth to this most wondrous Cause and to extirpate every lingering trace of that corrupt ecclesiastical hierarchy that has stained the fair name of Islám.'

The Báb replied:

'May God requite you for your noble intentions. So lofty a purpose is to Me even more precious than the act itself. Your days and Mine are numbered, however; they are too short to enable Me to witness, and allow you to achieve, the realisation of your hopes. Not by the means which you fondly imagine will an almighty Providence accomplish the triumph of His Faith. Through the poor and lowly of this land, by the blood which these shall have shed in His path, will the omnipotent Sovereign ensure the preservation and consolidate the foundation of His Cause. That same God will, in the world to come, place upon your head the crown of immortal glory, and will shower upon you His inestimable blessings. Of the span of your earthly life there remain only three months and nine days, after which you shall, with faith and certitude, hasten to your eternal abode.'

Manúchihr Khán marvelled and rejoiced at these words. He had come to realise that his vast wealth was the product of oppression. He repented that this was so and offered all that he possessed to the Báb, even taking the jewelled rings that he wore off his fingers. The Báb accepted both his repentance and his wealth and returned the riches to him for his use until his death. Strengthened and comforted, Manúchihr Khán settled all his private affairs and wrote a testament leaving all his wealth and possessions to the Báb. He spent more and more time in the presence of the Báb and gradually gained more insight into the message he had accepted.

'As the hour of my departure approaches', he told the Báb, 'I feel an undefinable joy pervading my soul. But I am apprehensive for You, I tremble at the thought of being compelled to leave You to the mercy of so ruthless a successor as Gurgín Khán. He will, no doubt, discover Your presence in this home, and will, I fear, grievously ill-treat You.'

Gurgín Khán was the nephew of Manúchihr Khán and his successor.

'Fear not,' the Báb told the governor, 'I have committed Myself into the hands of God. My trust is in Him . . . Of My own will have I chosen to be afflicted by My enemies . . .'

The governor died peacefully on the day foretold by the Báb. When his successor, Gurgín Khán, found out that the Báb had been a guest in the governor's house for four months, he at once notified the Sháh. The Sháh's confidence in Manúchihr Khán was not shaken for he was certain that the governor had only been waiting for a favourable time to bring the Báb to him. He gave orders for the Báb to be brought swiftly and secretly to Ṭihrán.

VI

Ká<u>sh</u>án to Tabríz

March 1847 – July 1847

CHAPTER 20

A SECRET SUMMONS TO ṬIHRÁN

The Sháh gave orders that Muḥammad Big, who held the post of chief courier, escort the Báb to Ṭihrán. Muḥammad Big belonged to the sect of Islám which is commonly known as the ‘Alíyu’lláhí, who are respected for their tolerance and upright conduct. The group of horsemen who were to act as a mounted escort for the Báb belonged to the Nuṣayrí sect which is very similar to the ‘Alíyu’lláhí. Gurgín Khán relayed to Muḥammad Big the Sháh’s exact instructions.

‘Beware lest anyone discover his identity or suspect the nature of your mission. No one but you, not even the members of his escort, should be allowed to recognise him. Should anyone question you concerning him, say that he is a merchant whom we have been instructed to conduct to the capital and of whose identity we are completely ignorant.’

The Báb was escorted out of Iṣfáhán under cover of darkness and as day broke the little group moved slowly northwards towards Ṭihrán. Behind them, to the south and west rose the Bakhtíarí ranges of the Zagros mountains while to their east lay the edges of the Dasht-i-Kavír, the great salt desert of central Persia.

The first town they approached was Káshán. Ḥájí Mírzá Jání, a noted merchant of Káshán, had accepted the message of the Báb when Mullá Ḥusayn had passed through on his first journey of teaching. Ḥájí Mírzá Jání had never seen the Báb and had no idea that He was on His way to Káshán, but as the Báb and His escort drew near, Ḥájí Mírzá Jání dreamed a remarkable dream.

In his dream he saw the Báb, dressed as a merchant, at the gate of Káshán. On the morning after he dreamed this dream, which was the eve of Naw-Rúz 1847, Ḥájí Mírzá Jání eagerly prepared his house for the coming of an honoured guest, dressed himself in his best clothes and went to wait at the town gate.

As he waited there, Ḥájí Mírzá Jání saw the Báb approaching and heard Him speak the words that He had spoken in the dream:

'We are to be your Guest for three nights,' said the Báb. 'Tomorrow is the day of Naw-Rúz, we shall celebrate it together in your home.'

With joy and wonder, Ḥájí Mírzá Jání moved forward to kiss the stirrup of the Báb. When Muḥammad Big, who was riding close to the Báb, saw Him greet Ḥájí Mírzá Jání, it seemed to him that they had known each other for a long time and he at once agreed to let the Báb spend Naw-Rúz with the merchant. But one of his fellow officers objected strongly to this decision, pointing out that their instructions were that they should not allow the Báb to enter any city on the way to Ṭihrán. There was a heated argument and Muḥammad Big finally persuaded his fellow officer that they should allow the Báb to stay with Ḥájí Mírzá Jání for three nights and that He should return to them on the third morning.

Ḥájí Mírzá Jání was eager to extend his hospitality to the entire party but the Báb dissuaded him from this. Ḥájí Mírzá Jání then asked to be allowed to at least pay for the upkeep of the escort while they were in Káshán.

'It is unnecessary,' the Báb told him, 'but for My will, nothing whatever could have induced them to deliver Me into your hands. All things lie prisoned within the grasp of His might. Nothing is impossible to Him. He removes every difficulty and surmounts every obstacle.'

The Báb spent Naw-Rúz quietly at the home of Ḥájí

Mírzá Jání and on the third morning returned to His escort. They continued northward towards Qum.

By the time the little cavalcade was approaching Qum, the Báb had won the hearts of all who escorted Him even though only Muḥammad Big knew His identity. His compelling dignity, alluring charm and unfailing kindness had lighted such devotion in the soldiers' hearts that, had He chosen to leave them, they would not have prevented Him, for they wanted only to serve and please Him. They had been ordered to keep well away from Qum but they said to the Báb:

'We have been particularly directed to keep away . . . We are ready, however, to ignore utterly for Your sake whatever instructions we have received. If it be Your wish, we shall unhesitatingly conduct You through the streets of Qum and enable You to visit its holy shrine.'

The Báb declined their offer:

'The heart of the true believer', He said, 'is the throne of God. He who is the ark of salvation and the Almighty's impregnable stronghold is now journeying with you through this wilderness. I prefer the way of the country rather than to enter this unholy city.'

They continued a short distance past Qum to the village of Qumrúd. The owner of Qumrúd was a relative of Muḥammad Big and the people of the village were of the 'Alíyu'lláhí sect. The headman of the village invited the Báb to stay one night with them and gave Him a kind and gracious welcome. The Báb was delighted with the warmth and spontaneity of the hospitality He was given and as He left them the next morning He cheered their hearts with words of gratitude and blessing.

The road from Qum to Ṭihrán passes very near to the desert. It is an inhospitable stretch of country, the days are hot and cloudless and the nights cold. After two more days of travelling, the Báb and His escort reached the fortress of

Kinár-Gard, which was only twenty-eight miles from Ṭihrán. The long journey from Iṣfáhán was almost over and they expected to be in the capital on the following day. But on that same evening a messenger arrived unexpectedly from Ṭihrán bringing a letter for Muḥammad Big from the Grand Vizier, Ḥájí Mírzá Áqásí.

CHAPTER 21

THE GRAND VIZIER PLAYS FOR TIME

When Muḥammad Big broke the seal of the letter from the Grand Vizier which was delivered to him at Kinár-Gard, he found that it contained orders to take the Báb immediately to the village of Kulayn. Ḥájí Mírzá Áqásí, the Grand Vizier, was so fearful of what might happen if the Báb were allowed to meet the Sháh that he had determined to prevent such a meeting by whatever means he could. He owned the village of Kulayn, which is situated to the west of Ṭihrán. The Grand Vizier ordered that the tent which was normally erected for him whenever he visited the village be put up for the Báb in an orchard on the gentle slope of a hill. The green luxuriance of that peaceful spot and the gentle, constant murmuring of streams gave some rest and solace to the Báb after His long journey. He had often been overcome with sadness since leaving Shíráz and His companions had seen Him weep bitterly many times. The strain of separation from His family and the perils of His captivity and enforced travelling had brought lines of fatigue and sorrow to His face.

After two days at Kulayn, several of the Bábís who had met with Him on His journey north arrived and were able to stay in the neighbourhood. The Bábís of Ṭihrán soon heard that the Báb was at Kulayn and a few came out to the village bringing with them a sealed letter from Bahá'u'lláh and a few small gifts sent by Him to the Báb. When the Báb received this letter and these gifts, His gloom and sorrow lifted and His grief changed to praise and thanksgiving. His companions marvelled at the radiant light that shone from Him. The comfort and strength, joy and exultation which the letter of Bahá'u'lláh imparted to the Báb stayed with Him through the difficult months that lay ahead. He overwhelmed the bearer of that letter with gratitude.

The group of Bábís who had come from Ṭihrán stayed at Kulayn for several days, and one night they were woken by the sudden sound of galloping hooves. They soon learnt that the guards had found the Báb's tent empty and that they were all anxiously searching for Him. However, Muḥammad Big was not at all worried and tried to calm the fearful soldiers.

'Why feel disturbed?' he pleaded with them. 'Are not His magnanimity and nobleness of soul sufficiently established in your eyes to convince you that He will never, for the sake of His own safety, consent to involve others in embarrassment? He, no doubt, must have retired, in the silence of this moonlit night, to a place where He can seek undisturbed communion with God. He will unquestionably return to His tent. He will never desert us.'

In order to reassure his companions, Muḥammad Big began to walk along the road that led to Ṭihrán and the Bábís followed him. They had gone only a short way and the dim light of early morning was just beginning to grow around them when they saw the slight figure of the Báb coming towards them from the direction of Ṭihrán.

'Did you believe Me to have escaped?' He gently asked Muḥammad Big. In reply the soldier flung himself at the feet of the Báb. He replied,

'Far be it from me to entertain such thoughts.'

In the grey light of dawn the Báb's face shone with radiance and majesty. All were awed by the power that seemed to surround Him and no one dared to ask Him anything, for a feeling of profound reverence filled their souls. The Báb said nothing but walked calmly back to His tent.

When nearly three weeks had passed since they had arrived in Kulayn, the Báb wrote a letter to Muḥammad Sháh requesting a meeting with him. The Sháh was planning a journey and Ḥájí Mírzá Áqásí was quick to offer advice. This is the advice he gave.

'The royal cavalcade is on the point of starting, and to engage in such matters as the present will conduce to the disruption of the kingdom . . . The imperial train is prepared for travel, neither is there hindrance or impediment in view. There is no doubt that the presence of the Báb will be the cause of the gravest trouble and the greatest mischief.'

The Grand Vizier convinced the Sháh that if the Báb came to Ṭihrán the divines of the city would dispute with Him and that this would cause a popular disturbance. There had recently been a serious rebellion in the province of Khurásán and the Grand Vizier played on the Sháh's fears of further rebellions in the very heart of his kingdom. Having convinced the Sháh of the gravity of the situation, Ḥájí Mírzá Áqásí put forward his own plan:

'On the spur of the moment,' he advised the Sháh, 'the wisest plan is this:– to place this person in the castle of Máh-Kú during the period of absence of the royal train from the seat of the imperial throne, and to defer the obtaining of an audience to the time of return.'

The Sháh accepted the advice of his Grand Vizier and sent this reply to the Báb:

'Since the royal train is on the verge of departure from Ṭihrán, to meet in a befitting manner is impossible. Do you go to Máh-Kú and there abide and rest for a while, engaged in praying for our victorious state; and we have arranged that under all circumstances they shall show you attention and respect. When we return from travel we will summon you specially.'

CHAPTER 22

THE ROAD TO TABRÍZ

The Grand Vizier was relieved and delighted that the Sháh had consented to his plan for sending the Báb to the distant and isolated castle of Máh-Kú. His fears of losing his position or of being toppled from power as a result of the Báb's teachings abated, for he had successfully blocked the way for the Báb to enter Ṭihrán and meet the Sháh.

Ádhirbáyján province is in the extreme northwest of Persia where the frontier meets the borders of Iráq, Turkey and the Soviet Union. Máh-Kú is in the farthest northwest corner of the mountainous province near the Turkish border. The distance from Ṭihrán to Máh-Kú is as great as the distance that the Báb had already been compelled to travel from Shíráz to Ṭihrán.

Máh-Kú can only be reached from Ṭihrán by travelling first to Tabríz, the provincial capital. Muḥammad Big was given the task of escorting the Báb to Tabríz and was told to keep the Báb away from all the towns on the way. The Báb was allowed only two companions to be with Him while He was in Ádhirbáyján province and He asked two brothers, Siyyid Ḥusayn-i-Yazdí and Siyyid Ḥasan, to go with Him. The government allotted funds for the Báb's expenses on the journey but the Báb used His own money that he had earned in Shíráz and Búshihr and spent the government funds on the poor and needy.

As the Báb and His escort began the long journey to the northwest they passed Qazvín, the home town of Ṭáhirih, and halted at a village nearby. The Bábís of Qazvín, informed of the Báb's approach, came out to meet Him. The Báb gave them several letters to deliver, one for the Grand Vizier, one for the divines of Qazvín and a third for a prominent Shaykhí leader of Zanján who had been a great admirer of Siyyid Káẓim. To him the Báb wrote:

'He whose virtues the late siyyid unceasingly extolled, and to the approach of whose Revelation he continually alluded, is now revealed. I am that Promised One. Arise and deliver Me from the hand of the oppressor.'

The Báb had not at any time appealed to the Bábís to rescue Him. He knew that imprisonment and suffering were destined for Him, and that any rescue attempt by the Bábís themselves would unleash a cruel persecution of all His followers. In delivering this clear challenge to the Shaykhí leader he tested the sincerity of his belief in the teachings of Siyyid Káẓim and gave him an opportunity to make a significant response to the new Revelation.

This Shaykhí received the letter within a few days but he did nothing about it and left Zanján for Ṭihrán. Ḥujjat, the religious leader who had so unhesitatingly declared his belief in the Báb, was at that time under house arrest in Ṭihrán, an arrest demanded by the 'ulamás of Zanján. When he heard of the Báb's appeal for help, he wrote at once to the Bábís of Zanján, asking them to go and rescue the Báb. They responded immediately and with a number of Bábís from Ṭihrán and Qazvín, they set out to rescue the Báb.

They found the Báb and His escort at midnight. All the guards were asleep. They begged the Báb to escape with them at once. He thanked them very lovingly for their assistance but advised them to give up their project and return home.

'The mountains of Ádhirbáyján too have their claims,' He told them.

Once past Qazvín, the Báb and His escort wound their way

slowly towards the mountains. Tabríz can only be reached from the east by negotiating two steep and terrifying mountain passes. Most of Ádhirbáyján province is made up of high mountain ranges. There are enormous domed summits, sombre gorges, jagged peaks and dizzy clefts cut through the rocks by tumultous streams. In the valleys there is deep and fertile soil and, where there is shelter from the bitter winds, cultivation is greater than anywhere in Persia except the Caspian lowlands. The routes in the Zagros follow tortuous river valleys, climb to rolling, table-like plateaux at high altitudes and then plunge to lower levels along precarious pathways.

The Báb might have escaped from His escort on many occasions during the journey but did not choose to do so. Once, near Tabríz, He galloped swiftly ahead of His escort and all the soldiers were amazed that the Báb's mount, which was the leanest of all the horses, could go so fast. They galloped after Him, but despite all their efforts they could not catch up with Him. Many times the soldiers were so tired that they were hardly able to remain in their saddles, but the Báb seemed tireless and rode as straight as an arrow, scarcely changing His posture for many hours and showing no trace of fatigue.

Before they reached Tabríz, Muḥammad Big acknowledged his belief in the Báb. He felt that he had not cared for the Báb on the journey as he ought to have done and in sorrow said to Him:

'The journey from Iṣfáhán has been long and arduous. I have failed to do my duty and to serve You as I ought. I crave Your forgiveness, and pray You to vouchsafe me Your blessings.'

The Báb replied lovingly.

'Be assured. I account you a member of My fold. They who embrace My Cause will eternally bless and glorify you, will extol your conduct and exalt your name.'

All the guards followed the example of Muḥammad Big in imploring the blessings of their prisoner. They kissed the feet of the Báb and with tearful eyes bade Him a last farewell. The Báb thanked them all and assured them of His prayers. Then they set their horses forward on the last stage of the journey to Tabríz where the Crown Prince, who was the governor of the great province of Á<u>dh</u>irbáyján, was waiting for the Báb to be delivered into his custody.

CHAPTER 23
INTO CUSTODY

As news of the Báb's approach spread in and around Tabríz, the Bábís from nearby villages tried to go and meet Him but were stopped by the governor's soldiers and sent back. Only one youth managed to evade the guards and ran, barefoot, for more than a mile along the road towards the small cavalcade. He threw himself in the path of one of the Báb's guards, caught the hem of the soldier's cloak, kissed his stirrups and cried out to all the astonished guards:

'Ye are the companions of my Well-Beloved. I cherish you as the apple of my eye.'

The soldiers were so astounded that they allowed the youth to approach the Báb. When he saw the Báb, he fell on the ground on his face and wept. The Báb dismounted from His horse, raised him up from the ground, comforted him and wiped away his tears.

A great crowd of people had gathered near the city gates in order to see the Báb enter Tabríz. The city of Tabríz is a proud and bustling place but it is markedly different from the warm, southern city of Shíráz, the birth-place of the Báb. The Tabríz area is frequently shaken by earthquakes which have destroyed most of the city's old buildings and there are few gardens, fountains or shady areas as water is scarce.

The news of the Báb's approach caused such an uproar in the city that a crier was ordered to warn of the dangers facing anyone who tried to see the Báb. The crier called out:

'Whosoever shall make any attempt to approach the Siyyid-i-Báb or seek to meet him, all his possessions shall forthwith be seized and he himself condemned to perpetual imprisonment.'

This stern warning did not deter the people. Thousands watched as the Báb was brought into their city. Some were merely curious, others were moved by what they saw to investigate His claim and some, already His followers, kissed the dust of His footsteps. The Báb was led through the crowded streets to one of the principal houses of the city which was allotted for His use. A detachment of soldiers was ordered to guard the door and only Siyyid Ḥusayn and Siyyid Ḥasan were allowed to remain with Him. Neither His followers nor any members of the public were allowed to see Him.

There was a Bábí in Tabríz named Ḥájí 'Alí-Askar. This man had long regretted that he had not seen the Báb in Shíráz. Ḥájí 'Alí-Askar had accompanied Mullá Ḥusayn from Shíráz to Mashhad and had often shared with him the great sorrow he felt in never having been in the presence of the Báb.

'Grieve not,' Mullá Ḥusayn had told him confidently. 'The Almighty is no doubt able to compensate you in Tabríz for the loss you have sustained in Shíráz. Not once, but seven times, can He enable you to partake of the joy of His presence, in return for the one visit which you have missed.'

Ḥájí 'Alí-Askar had been very astonished at this confident reply but soon forgot about the conversation.

The day after the Báb reached Tabríz, Ḥájí 'Alí-Askar, together with a prominent Bábí of Tabríz, approached the house where the Báb was confined. The friends of these two had warned them that they were putting not only their possessions but their lives at risk in attempting to see the Báb. As they reached the house, soldiers moved forward and arrested them. Just then Siyyid Ḥasan came out of the house.

'I am commanded by the Siyyid-i-Báb', he told the guards,

'to convey to you this message: "Suffer these visitors to enter, inasmuch as I Myself have invited them to meet Me."'

The guards were silent and subdued and allowed the two visitors into the house where the Báb greeted His guests and said:

'These miserable wretches who watch at the gate of My house have been destined by Me as a protection against the inrush of the multitude who throng around the house. They are powerless to prevent those whom I desire to meet from attaining My presence.'

Ḥájí 'Alí-Askar and his companion stayed about two hours with the Báb, and as they left the Báb assured him that if he desired to come again, no one would prevent him. Ḥájí 'Alí-Askar visited the Báb a number of times but it was during his seventh visit that the words which Mullá Ḥusayn had earlier spoken to him on the journey to Mashhad came sharply to his mind, as he heard the Báb say to him:

'Praise be to God, who has enabled you to complete the number of your visits and who has extended to you His loving protection.'

One day, Siyyid Ḥusayn ventured to ask the Báb how long He would continue to remain in Tabríz or whether He would be transferred to another place.

'Have you forgotten', the Báb replied, 'the question you asked me in Iṣfáhán? For a period of no less than nine months, we shall remain confined in the Jabal-i-Básiṭ,[1] from whence we shall be transferred to the Jabal-i-Shadíd.[2] Both these places are among the mountains of Khuy and are situated on either side of the town bearing that name.'

Five days later, orders were issued to transfer the Báb to the castle of Máh-Kú.

1. The Open Mountain. 2. The Grievous Mountain. These are names given by the Báb to the places of His imprisonment.

VII

Máh-Kú

July 1847 – April 1848

CHAPTER 24
A STRICT CONFINEMENT

Forty days after His arrival at Tabríz, the Báb was escorted out of the city and another stage of His enforced journey began. The small cavalcade followed the slow and difficult road north, past the town of Khuy and northwards again, across desolate high plains and along a dangerous mountain pass towards the town and castle of Máh-Kú.

The plains around Máh-Kú are dotted with outcrops of black volcanic rock which rise like stark waves of a black and frozen sea. The rocks of the narrow pass are twisted and contorted by aeons of violent volcanic upheaval and by the constant weathering of wind and water. The river Araxes, which runs in a major volcanic fault structure to the west of the town, forms the frontier with Turkey. The poet Ḥáfiẓ wrote of this harsh land and of the Báb's presence in it, centuries ago, in the warm southern gardens of Shíráz:

'*O zephyr, shouldst thou pass by the banks of the Araxes, implant a kiss on the earth of that valley and make fragrant thy breath.*'

The only way to reach the castle of Máh-Kú is through the small town of the same name which straggles up the steep hillside towards it. A stream gushes out from the rocks below the castle and the path is twisting and treacherous. The castle, a solid building with four strong towers, dominates the town and is in its turn dominated by an enormous, menacing mountain shaped like a great bow, which rises above it. A massive overhanging rock leans heavily upwards and outwards right above the castle and the town, broken only by one jagged cleft which falls crookedly, for hundreds of feet, from the summit. Neither rain nor snow can fall on the castle roof because of this overhang, nor can the stars be seen at night. In summer the heat is tremendous, for the mountains gather it into their rocky sides in the daytime and reflect it back through the stifling nights. In winter the sunlight cannot reach the icebound rocks which lie under the overhang, and the air is always chill.

Máh-Kú was the birthplace of Ḥájí Mírzá Áqásí, and the Grand Vizier was a figure of considerable power and influence in the area. Ḥájí Mírzá Áqásí knew that he could normally rely completely on the loyalty and obedience of the people of Máh-Kú. The local people are Kurdish and they belong to the Sunní sect of Islám: they detest the Shí‘ih Moslems and have a particularly strong hatred for the siyyids, the descendants of the family of Muḥammad.

Ḥájí Mírzá Áqásí believed that few, if any, of the Bábís would dare to venture into this remote, inhospitable and dangerously-situated corner of Persia and that, isolated from His followers, the influence of the Báb would speedily dwindle and die altogether. He gave orders that the Báb should be kept in strict confinement and that absolutely no one should be allowed to visit Him.

The governor of the prison, ‘Alí Khán, himself half Kurdish, was a rough and simple man who was anxious to please the Grand Vizier. He followed his instructions carefully, kept the Báb in strict confinement and allowed only the two brothers, Siyyid Ḥusayn and Siyyid Ḥasan, to be with Him. The Báb was denied even a candle to light His doorless, mud-walled cell, and the only other occupants of the entire castle were two guards and four dogs. A Bábí named Shaykh Ḥasan-i-Zunúzí, seeking the presence of the Báb, soon reached Máh-Kú but ‘Alí Khán would not allow him to stay in the town, not even for one night. Shaykh

Ḥasan was forced to seek shelter in a small mosque a short way from the town.

Despite the strictness of His confinement, the influence of the Báb was felt in Máh-Kú from the moment of His arrival. The guards reported on the extraordinary character of their Prisoner; they told the townspeople of His gentle charm, His wisdom and His tender love. Soon the peasant farmers of the area began to gather each day beneath the castle walls, anxious for a glimpse of Him. They begged for His blessing on their daily work and when they quarrelled or had disputes to settle, they implored each other beneath the castle walls, to tell the truth in His name. 'Alí Khán tried hard to stop them but he could not. Other Bábís now reached Máh-Kú but they were only able to relay messages to the Báb through Shaykh Ḥasan from his shelter at the mosque outside the town. He passed the messages to Siyyid Ḥasan, the Báb's secretary, who came from the castle to the town each day in order to fetch necessary supplies.

After a few weeks had passed in this way, the Báb told Siyyid Ḥasan to inform Shaykh Ḥasan that He would himself ask 'Alí Khán to change his attitude to the Bábís who came to Máh-Kú. Siyyid Ḥasan contained the surprise he felt at the Báb's words and did as he was asked. Early the next morning before anyone was awake in the castle, a furious knocking began at the castle gate. The guards were startled, for they had been given orders that no one was to enter before sunrise. They were even more startled to hear the voice of the warden of the castle, 'Alí Khán himself, calling them to open the door.

CHAPTER 25
THE PRISON DOORS OPEN

When the startled guards hurriedly opened the castle gates, they were astonished to see 'Alí Khán standing submissively on the threshold, his face expressing humility and wonder. Very courteously, he begged to be allowed to enter the presence of his Prisoner. He could not hide his agitation: his hands shook and his limbs trembled as he walked towards the Báb's prison cell. The Báb rose to receive him and 'Alí Khán bowed reverently and flung himself at His feet.

'Deliver me from my perplexity,' he pleaded. 'I adjure You, by the Prophet of God, Your illustrious Ancestor, to dissipate my doubts, for their weight has well-nigh crushed my heart. I was riding through the wilderness and was approaching the gate of the town, when, it being the hour of dawn, my eyes suddenly beheld You standing by the side of the river engaged in offering Your prayer. With outstretched arms and upraised eyes You were invoking the name of God. I stood still and watched You. I was waiting for You to terminate Your devotions that I might approach and rebuke You for having ventured to leave the castle without my leave. In Your communion with God, You seemed so wrapt in worship that You were utterly forgetful of Yourself. I quietly approached You; in Your state of rapture, You remained wholly unaware of my presence. I was suddenly seized with great fear and recoiled at the thought of awakening You from Your ecstasy. I decided to leave You, to proceed to the guards and reprove them for their negligent conduct. I soon found out, to my amazement, that both the outer and inner gates were closed. They were opened at my request, I was ushered into Your presence and now find You, to my wonder, seated before me. I am utterly confounded. I know not whether my reason has deserted me.'

The Báb answered:

'What you have witnessed is true and undeniable. You belittled this Revelation and have contemptuously disdained its Author. God, the All-Merciful, desiring not to afflict you with His punishment, has willed to reveal to your eyes the Truth. By His Divine interposition, He has instilled into your heart the love of His chosen One, and caused you to recognise the unconquerable power of His Faith.'

'Alí Khán humbly begged the Báb to grant him a request:

'A poor man, a shaykh,' he told the Báb, 'is yearning to attain Your presence. He lives in a masjid outside the gate of Máh-Kú. I pray You that I myself be allowed to bring him to this place that he may meet You. By this act I hope that my evil deeds may be forgiven, that I may be enabled to wash away the stains of my cruel behaviour towards Your friends.'

The Báb granted his request and 'Alí Khán hurried away to bring Shaykh Ḥasan to the Báb. 'Alí Khán became, from that day, so devoted to the Báb that he did all he could to make the Báb's time in the prison more tolerable. He presented Him with gifts of the choicest fruit available in the neighbourhood and he came every Friday to pay Him a respectful visit. The castle gates were still locked at night but in the daytime all were allowed access. Many Bábís began to travel to Máh-Kú from all parts of Persia. The Báb allowed each pilgrim to stay for three days and then sent them away with instructions to carry on the teaching work.

It was many weeks before any reports of these events at Máh-Kú could be carried to Ṭihrán by the spies of Ḥájí Mírzá Áqásí. When the Grand Vizier first heard these reports, he was bewildered and furious that such events could occur in his own birthplace. He fumed and raged in helpless frustration and struggled to think what action he should take next. He had been unable to isolate the Báb from His followers, and in his attempt to do so he had unwittingly been the cause of introducing the person and the teachings of the Báb to his own birthplace. He had, moreover, unintentionally, by isolating the Báb from His family and relatives, provided Him with the comparative peace necessary for Him to reveal and record His teachings. The Báb, conscious that He had only a few years of earthly life left to Him, did all that He could to teach His followers while He was still with them.

CHAPTER 26
THE BÁB SETS DOWN HIS TEACHINGS

In the nine months that He spent at Máh-Kú the Báb revealed many of His writings. He Himself stated that up to the time of His imprisonment at Máh-Kú, He had already revealed more than five hundred thousand verses. Many of these writings had already been destroyed by people fearful of what might happen to them if they were found with writings of the Báb in their possession.

Shaykh Ḥasan, the first Bábí to reach Máh-Kú, has left this dramatic account of the scene at Máh-Kú as the Báb revealed His writings:

'The voice of the Báb, as He dictated the teachings and principles of His Faith, could be clearly heard by those who were dwelling at the foot of the mountain. The melody of His chanting, the rhythmic flow of the verses which streamed from His lips caught our ears and penetrated into our very souls. Mountain and valley re-echoed the majesty of His voice. Our hearts vibrated in their depths to the appeal of His utterance.'

During these months, the Báb revealed nine separate commentaries on the Holy Qur'án. The fate of all these commentaries is unknown, but it is certain that one of them was a work equalling in importance the commentary on the Súrih of Joseph which the Báb had revealed on the night He declared His mission. He wrote several important letters to Muḥammad Sháh, to the divines of every city in Persia and also to the divines of Karbilá and Najaf. He revealed a book called 'The Seven Proofs', wrote the Arabic Bayán and began work on the Persian Bayán. The Arabic Bayán is the shorter of the two books: the Persian Bayán contains eight thousand verses and is the Báb's single most important work.

The name Bayán means Utterance. In the Bayán, the Báb cancels the laws given by Muḥammad which relate to the practices of prayer, fasting, marriage, divorce and inheritance but firmly upholds belief in the prophetic mission of Muḥammad. He reveals the laws necessary for His own brief dispensation and explains that when 'He Whom God shall make manifest' will appear, He will either approve or alter any or all of the laws which He, the Báb, has revealed. He explains the meaning of many theological terms such as Paradise, Hell, Death, Resurrection, the Return, the Hour and the Last Judgement. He neither names a successor nor appoints an interpreter of His teachings. The single most important fact about the Bayán is that it is written in praise of 'Him Whom God shall make manifest'. Addressing Him, the Báb writes:

'. . . the Bayán and such as bear allegiance to it are but a present from me unto Thee.'

The Báb explains in the Bayán that every revealed religion passes through the stages of birth, of growth and of yielding its most perfect fruit. In writing of the 'Day of Resurrection' the Báb explains that this 'Day of Resurrection' occurs each time that a new Messenger of God appears.

'For example, from the inception of the mission of Jesus – may peace be upon Him – till the day of His ascension was the Resurrection of Moses . . . And from the moment when the Tree of the Bayán appeared until it disappeareth is the Resurrection of the Apostle of God [Muḥammad], as is divinely foretold in the Qur'án . . . The stage of perfection of everything is reached when its resurrection occurreth . . . The Resurrection of the Bayán will occur at the time of the appearance of Him Whom God shall make manifest. For today the Bayán is in the stage of seed: at the beginning of the manifestation of Him Whom God shall make manifest its ultimate perfection will become apparent . . .'

The Báb repeatedly warns his followers lest they fail to recognise the One Whose coming He Himself foretells:

'Suffer not the Bayán and all that hath been revealed therein to withhold you from that Essence of Being and Lord of the visible and invisible . . . Better is it for thee to recite but one of the verses of Him Whom God shall make manifest than to set down the whole of the Bayán, for on that Day that one verse can save thee, whereas the entire Bayán cannot save thee.'

Almost all the Báb's written references to 'Him Whom God shall make manifest' date from the period of His captivity in Ádhirbáyján. He assured some of His own disciples that they would themselves attain His presence and He warned them all:

'O people of the Bayán! Be on your guard . . . He will shine forth suddenly . . . purge thou thine ear . . . thine eye . . . thy conscience . . . thy tongue . . . thy hand . . . thy knowledge . . . thy heart . . . and . . . purge all thine acts and thy pursuits that thou mayest be nurtured in the paradise of pure love, and perchance mayest attain the presence of Him Whom God shall make manifest adorned with a purity which He highly cherisheth.'

The Bayán contains countless references and allusions, some clear and others deliberately obscure, to 'Him Whom God shall make manifest'. Addressing the Beloved of His heart, the One for Whom the Báb is preparing to give His own life, He writes:

'. . . do Thou grant a respite of nineteen years as a token of Thy favour so that those who have embraced this Cause may be graciously rewarded by Thee.'

The third Vaḥíd (Unity) of the Bayán contains this emphatic and prophetic sentence:

'Well is it with him who fixeth his gaze upon the Order of Bahá'u'lláh, and rendereth thanks unto his Lord. For He will assuredly be made manifest. God hath indeed irrevocably ordained it in the Bayán.'

The summer and autumn of 1847 passed with a constant stream of Bábí pilgrims reaching Máh-Kú. The winter of that year was so severe that the copper pots and pans used in the castle were damaged by the intense cold and the water which the Báb used for His ablutions froze on His face. During these cold months the Báb asked Siyyid Ḥasan to read aloud to Him a celebrated account of the martyrdom of the Imám Ḥusayn, the grandson of Muḥammad, who was murdered on the plain of Karbilá. As He listened, the Báb wept bitterly for the cruel treatment given to the Imám Ḥusayn and for the more grievous sufferings which the Ḥusayn Who would shortly appear (Bahá'u'lláh) would have to bear.

CHAPTER 27

MULLÁ ḤUSAYN VISITS MÁH-KÚ

While the Báb remained a prisoner at Máh-Kú, the Sháh, who had sent Him there on the advice of his Grand Vizier, was encountering grave problems. Khurásán province, where disturbances had occurred repeatedly since 1844, was again in disorder. A group of local leaders rebelled against the central government and a large government force sent from Ṭihrán to subdue them was defeated.

Mullá Ḥusayn was living in Mashhad at the time. The chief of the rebels tried to involve him in their activities and contacted him with a plea for assistance. Mullá Ḥusayn did not want to be involved in the plots of the rebellious chief and as soon as he received this letter he quietly left Mashhad at night with one companion. His friends hurried after him as soon as they heard of his departure, but when they caught up with him, Mullá Ḥusayn declined all their offers of help:

'I have vowed', he said, 'to walk the whole distance that separates me from my Beloved. I shall not relax in my resolve until I shall have reached my destination.'

Mashhad lies far in the east of Persia and Máh-Kú is in the furthest northwest corner of the country. The distance between the two places is at least nine hundred miles.

Mullá Ḥusayn even tried to persuade his one companion, Qambar-'Alí, to return to Mashhad but finally consented to allow him to act as his servant during the journey. As he walked westwards, the Bábís in the villages and towns through which he passed greeted him with enthusiasm and repeatedly offered him help which he repeatedly declined.

His ardent faith and complete steadfastness inspired everyone he met. In Ṭihrán he was secretly taken to see Bahá'u'lláh and then continued on his way to Ádhirbáyján. On the eve of Naw-Rúz 1848, he was only one day's journey from Máh-Kú.

That night, 'Alí Khán, the warden of the castle, dreamed a strange dream. He later recounted it:

'In my sleep, I was startled by the sudden intelligence that Muḥammad, the Prophet of God, was soon to arrive at Máh-Kú . . . In my dream, I ran out to meet Him, eager to extend to so holy a Visitor the expression of my humble welcome. In a state of indescribable gladness, I hastened on foot in the direction of the river, and as I reached the bridge . . . I saw two men advancing towards me. I thought one of them to be the Prophet Himself, while the other who walked behind Him, I supposed to be one of His distinguished companions. I hastened to throw myself at His feet, and was bending to kiss the hem of His robe, when I suddenly awoke. A great joy had flooded my soul. I felt as if Paradise itself, with all its delights, had been crowded into my heart.'

'Alí Khán got up, said his morning prayers, dressed in his best clothes and hurried down to the bridge below the town. He ordered his servants to saddle his three best and swiftest horses and to bring them after him. It was sunrise as he reached the bridge. There, with a throb of wonder, 'Alí Khán saw the two figures of his dream approaching. He fell at the feet of Mullá Ḥusayn and kissed them, begging him and his companion to ride the horses which he had prepared for them. Mullá Ḥusayn declined his offer:

'I have vowed to accomplish the whole of my journey on foot. I will walk to the summit of this mountain and will there visit your Prisoner.'

Wondering greatly, 'Alí Khán followed Mullá Ḥusayn on foot up to the gate of the castle where the Báb was waiting just inside the gate. When Mullá Ḥusayn first saw the Báb he halted instantly, bowed low before Him and then stood still by His side. The Báb embraced him affectionately and led him by the hand to His room. He called others to Him, a feast of choice dishes and fruits was spread before them and together they celebrated the Feast of Naw-Rúz.

Up to that time, no one but the two companions of the Báb who had come with Him from Tabríz had been allowed to sleep at the castle, but on that day 'Alí Khán, whose devotion to the Báb was increased greatly by his strange and mystical experience, said to Him:

'If it be Your desire to retain Mullá Ḥusayn with You this night, I am ready to abide by Your wish, for I have no will of my own. However long You desire him to stay with You, I pledge myself to carry out Your command.'

From that day, the Bábís reached Máh-Kú in even greater numbers and no restrictions were placed on them.

One day, when the Báb and Mullá Ḥusayn were looking out over the surrounding land from the roof of the castle, the Báb spoke these words to him:

'The days of your stay in this country are approaching their end . . . A few days after your departure from this place they will transfer Us to another mountain. Ere you arrive at your destination, the news of Our departure from Máh-Kú will have reached you.'

The Báb then told Mullá Ḥusayn all that must happen to Him but commanded him not to repeat what he heard to anyone. He directed Mullá Ḥusayn to travel to Tabríz and other parts of Ádhirbáyján first, to visit next Zanján, Qazvín, Ṭihrán and, finally, to proceed to the province of Mázindarán. The Báb gave him no assurance that they would meet again in this world but bade him a tender farewell:

'You have walked on foot all the way from your native province to this place. On foot you likewise must return . . .

for your days of horsemanship are yet to come. You are destined to exhibit such courage, such skill and heroism as shall eclipse the mightiest deeds of the heroes of old. Your daring exploits will win the praise and admiration of the dwellers in the eternal Kingdom. You should visit, on your way, the believers . . . To each you will convey the expression of My love and tender affection. You will strive to inflame their hearts anew with the fire of the love of the Beauty of God, and will endeavour to fortify their faith in His Revelation. From Ṭihrán you should proceed to Mázindarán, where God's hidden treasure will be made manifest to you. You will be called upon to perform deeds so great as will dwarf the mightiest achievements of the past. The nature of your task will, in that place, be revealed to you, and strength and guidance will be bestowed upon you that you may be fitted to render your service to His Cause.'

Nine days after he had reached Máh-Kú, Mullá Ḥusayn left the castle and the town.

The government spies who were stationed in Máh-Kú were by this time sending the most alarming reports to the Grand Vizier. They wrote of the increasing numbers of Bábí pilgrims and of the increased devotion of 'Alí Khán to his Prisoner. They wrote that 'Alí Khán, who had refused to allow his daughter to marry the Crown Prince, now begged the Báb to accept that same daughter in marriage. 'Alí Khán begged Mullá Ḥusayn to intercede on his behalf in this matter but the Báb firmly refused.

The Russian minister in Ṭihrán was also alarmed by the presence of the Báb so near to the Russian border. Only a few years earlier, a certain mullá in the area had proclaimed the advent of the Hidden Imám and within one month had gathered to his cause thirty thousand followers. The Russians had been seriously disturbed by this event and had no wish to see it happen again.

The Grand Vizier was bitterly resentful of the way in which his plans had gone awry. He became afraid of what might happen if the Báb remained at Máh-Kú and sent a sudden order that the Báb be transferred immediately to Chihríq. Eleven days after Mullá Ḥusayn left Máh-Kú in early April 1848, the Báb too left the Open Mountain of Máh-Kú and was taken to the Grievous Mountain, the grim fortress of Chihríq.

VIII

Chihríq

April 1848 – September 1848

CHAPTER 28

ANOTHER STRICT CONFINEMENT FAILS

The castle of Chihríq is south of the town of Khuy and to the west of Lake Riḍá'íyyih in an area famous as the birthplace of Zoroaster, an earlier Messenger of God. It is a desolate place: the castle stands gloomily at the foot of a steep crag in barren countryside. The prison warden, a Kurdish chieftain named Yaḥyá Khán, was a brother-in-law of Muḥammad Sháh. Yaḥyá Khán was ordered to keep the Báb in strict confinement and to allow Him no visitors. The Grand Vizier specifically warned Yaḥyá Khán not to follow the lamentable example of 'Alí Khán, warden of the castle of Má-Kú.

Yaḥyá Khán was known to be a harsh man but after only a short while he found himself quite unable to obey his orders, for the love of the Báb penetrated his heart and captivated his entire being. He refused no one access to the castle and the little town of Chihríq became so crowded that the Bábí pilgrims had to stay at another small town one hour's journey away. The local Kurdish people were known to hate the Shí'ih Muslims even more fiercely than did the people of Máh-Kú, yet they too quickly became devoted to the Báb. At daybreak they came to the castle to beg His blessing on their work and in the evenings they told each other all the stories they could learn of the holy Prisoner of Chihríq.

The inhabitants of Khuy travelled to Chihríq to see the Báb, and soon a number of the religious teachers and government officials in Khuy became Bábís. However, there was one man in Khuy, a well-respected government official named Mírzá Asadu'lláh, who opposed the new teachings vigorously and was determined that no one should succeed in converting him to the faith of the Báb. Mírzá Asadu'lláh held an important post and was renowned for his great learning and fluent prose.

One night Mírzá Asadu'llah had a strange dream which prompted him to write a letter to the Báb. When the reply came Mírzá Asadu'lláh immediately hurried on foot to C͟hihríq, attained the presence of the Báb, accepted His teachings with his whole heart and at once began to teach others with great enthusiasm. He wrote a remarkable treatise proving the validity of the Báb's mission and the Báb bestowed upon him the name of Dayyán, which means Conqueror or Judge. Dayyán's father, who was a friend of the Grand Vizier, became so alarmed by his son's conversion that he wrote a full report of it to Ṭihrán.

One day a dervish, a holy man, arrived at C͟hihríq barefoot, poorly clothed and carrying only a staff and a begging bowl. He had walked all the way from India to C͟hihríq. No one knew, and still no one knows exactly who he was or where he came from. This is all he said of himself:

'In the days when I occupied the exalted position of navváb in India, the Báb appeared to me in a vision. He gazed at me and won my heart completely. I arose, and had started to follow Him, when He looked at me intently and said: "Divest yourself of your gorgeous attire, depart from your native land, and hasten on foot to meet Me in Ád͟hirbáyján. In C͟hihríq you will attain your heart's desire." I followed His directions and have now reached my goal.'

When his stay at C͟hihríq was ended, the Báb instructed the dervish to return to India as he had come and to teach the Faith there. The dervish refused to take even one companion with him, saying that as the Báb had instructed him to return alone, anyone else would perish on the journey. He refused gifts of food and clothing, set out alone with his staff and his bowl and no one knows what became of him. This incident was also fully reported to the Grand Vizier by the spies whom he had stationed at Chihríq.

While these reports were reaching him, the Grand Vizier had more than the Cause of the Báb to worry about. The Sháh's health was failing. Muḥammad Sháh was only forty but he suffered greatly from gout and was in very poor health as a result of this illness. Ḥájí Mírzá Áqásí knew that his own enemies at court were waiting, like jackals and vultures, for the death of the Sháh. He was painfully aware that they were already working to destroy his own power and seize all his possessions even as Muḥammad Sháh sank slowly towards death.

CHAPTER 29

THE LETTERS OF THE LIVING AND THE CONFERENCE OF BADASHT

While the Grand Vizier watched the Sháh's health deteriorate daily and while the Báb remained captive at Chihríq, the Báb's first disciples, the Letters of the Living, were exerting every effort to spread His teachings and to prepare every receptive heart for the coming of 'Him Whom God shall make manifest'.

After leaving the Báb at Máh-Kú, Mullá Ḥusayn had followed carefully the instructions given to him. He had visited the towns to which the Báb had directed him, had seen Bahá'u'lláh in Ṭihrán and then had headed north-east through the Elburz mountains to the province of Mázindarán which stretches along the south-east shores of the Caspian Sea. Mázindarán is a thickly populated and prosperous province. The farm land is fertile, there are fish in the streams and there is game in the dense jungles. There are few towns in the province but a multitude of farms and small hamlets. The Báb had promised Mullá Ḥusayn that he would find in Mázindarán 'a hidden treasure'.

Quddús had also been travelling and teaching since he had accompanied the Báb on pilgrimage to Mecca. Mullá Ḥusayn met Quddús at the small town of Bárfurúsh in Mázindarán. Quddús was born in Bárfurúsh and he was at that time living in his father's house.

Quddús welcomed Mullá Ḥusayn, listened eagerly to the news from Ádhirbáyján and asked if Mullá Ḥusayn had brought with him any of the Báb's writings. When Mullá

Ḥusayn replied that he had not, Quddús brought out a manuscript, gave it to Mullá Ḥusayn and asked him to read some parts of it. As soon as he read one page of that manuscript, Mullá Ḥusayn knew that he had already found 'the hidden treasure' in Mázindarán of which the Báb had spoken. He was startled and shaken by the power of the words he read. Putting down the manuscript he said:

'I can well realise that the Author of these words has drawn His inspiration from that Fountainhead which stands immeasurably superior to the sources whence the learning of men is ordinarily derived. I hereby testify to my wholehearted recognition of the sublimity of these words and to my unquestioned acceptance of the truth which they reveal.'

Quddús remained silent, and from both his silence and his expression Mullá Ḥusayn understood that he had himself written the manuscript. Mullá Ḥusayn rose from his seat and with bowed head reverently declared:

'The hidden treasure of which the Báb has spoken, now lies unveiled before my eyes. Its light has dispelled the gloom of perplexity and doubt. Though my Master be now hidden amid the mountain fastnesses of Ádhirbáyján, the sign of His splendour and the revelation of His might stand manifest before me. I have found in Mázindarán the reflection of His glory.'

Quddús asked Mullá Ḥusayn to go to Mashhad immediately and prepare a house for both of them to use as a base for their teaching work in the province. Mullá Ḥusayn went to Mashhad, bought a piece of land and built on it a house which he called the Bábíyyih. Quddús soon joined him there, and a wave of teaching swept over the city and through the entire province, the effects of which were felt far beyond the borders of Khurásán. From that time on, until the end of his life, Mullá Ḥusayn showed extreme deference and humility towards Quddús and carried out instantly whatever Quddús asked him to do.

While Quddús and Mullá Ḥusayn were teaching in Mashhad, the Báb wrote a letter to all the believers in Persia directing them to 'hasten to the Land of Khá' (Khurásán). News of the Báb's summons spread quickly through Persia and to Iráq, where Ṭáhirih was teaching. As soon as Ṭáhirih heard of the Báb's call, she prepared to leave. The divines of Karbilá and Baghdád tried to dissuade her but were unsuccessful. Undeterred by their counsels and warnings, she set out with a few companions across the desert and over the Zagros range to Hamadán. There she was met by a delegation sent from Qazvín by her father. They requested her to visit her father and to stay for a while in Qazvín. Ṭáhirih reluctantly agreed. When she arrived in Qazvín, Ṭáhirih refused to be reunited with her husband and went to live at her father's house.

Ṭáhirih's father-in-law, Ḥájí Mullá Taqí, who was also her uncle, was a prominent divine of Qazvín. He was hot-tempered and impetuous, rigidly narrow-minded in his traditionalist views and bitterly opposed to Shaykh Aḥmad and Siyyid Kázim. He frequently denounced their teachings from the pulpit in abusive language. He now began to attack the Bábís even more fiercely as he felt himself personally insulted by Ṭáhirih's actions. A man from Shíráz who was a fervent admirer of Shaykh Aḥmad and Siyyid Kázim became so incensed at the abuse heaped upon them and their teachings that he determined to kill Ḥájí Mullá Taqí. He bought a weapon, hid it in his clothing, watched and waited, and one morning, at dawn, he murdered him in the mosque.

Three Bábís of Qazvín who were completely innocent of the deed were accused of murder and were quickly executed. This was the first public execution of Bábís in the country and the three were the first Bábís to die as martyrs in Persia itself. Ṭáhirih was put under house arrest and her life was in danger. Bahá'u'lláh arranged for her rescue and her safe journey to Ṭihrán, but she stayed only a short while in Ṭihrán and went on to Khurásán as directed by the Báb.

In Mashhad, which had only recently recovered from a series of rebellions, Quddús and Mullá Ḥusayn were continuing to teach energetically and the large numbers of people visiting the Bábíyyih alarmed the authorities. The chief constable tried to stop them teaching. He arrested Ḥasan, Mullá Ḥusayn's servant, ordered that his nose be pierced and that he be led through the city on a halter. This order was carried out and it so enraged some of the Bábís that they rushed to rescue him. In the following confusion the men who were leading Ḥasan on a halter were killed and the city was again thrown into uproar.

When the Bábís took Ḥasan back to Mullá Ḥusayn, he reproached them sadly for what they had done.

'You have refused to tolerate the trials to which Ḥasan has been subjected,' he said. 'How can you reconcile yourselves to the martyrdom of Ḥusayn?'

Mullá Ḥusayn and his servant Ḥasan were named after Imám Ḥusayn and Imám Ḥasan, the two grandsons of Muḥammad who were brutally persecuted. Each year, the Persians commemorate the murder of Ḥusayn and mourn his loss. By reproaching his companions in this way, Mullá Ḥusayn attempted to make clear to them the gravity of the situation and to prepare them for his own approaching martyrdom.

A government commander, Prince Ḥamzih Mírzá, who was stationed with his soldiers a short distance outside Mashhad, summoned Mullá Ḥusayn to his camp. Quddús advised Mullá Ḥusayn to obey, saying that no harm could come of it. Mullá Ḥusayn left for the Prince's camp and Quddús set out to meet with the Bábís whom the Báb had directed to Khurásán and who were converging on the village of Badasht.

Eighty-one Bábís came to Badasht and stayed there as Bahá'u'lláh's guests for twenty-one days. The time that they spent there is now referred to as the Conference of Badasht, though of all those who arrived at Badasht, only Bahá'u'lláh and Quddús knew how important an event this gathering of Bábís at the tiny hamlet would prove to be.

In his book the Bayán, the Báb had clearly and definitely abrogated the laws of Muḥammad which related to prayer, fasting, marriage and divorce by which the lives of Muslims had been strictly governed for a thousand years. Some of the Bábís, while recognising the Báb and believing in Him, were continuing to observe the laws of Muḥammad in their daily lives. It was very difficult for some of them to even consider stepping outside the habitual security of these laws which had affected every day of their lives since their birth and which shaped the society of their country. However, their continuing observance of these laws prevented them from understanding that the Báb had inaugurated a new dispensation which was entirely separate from the dispensation of Muḥammad. Others amongst the Bábís saw clearly that the Báb had ushered in a new dispensation. They were eager to adopt the laws that He had brought and were impatient with their more traditionalist fellow believers.

Bahá'u'lláh and Quddús were aware that the time had come to resolve this issue and to demonstrate clearly that the Báb had brought a new and independent religion. They arranged for a dramatic confrontation between the two viewpoints to take place at which this truth would be evident and undeniable. Each day of the conference, Bahá'u'lláh revealed verses which were chanted to all present. Each day saw the abrogation of one of the laws of Islám. Bahá'u'lláh bestowed a new name upon each of the believers, a name by which each was addressed in letters written to each of them by the Báb and received shortly after the conference. No one amongst the guests suspected that Bahá'u'lláh was unobtrusively guiding the gathering towards a dramatic climax.

In the emerging confrontation, Quddús took the part of the traditionalists and Ṭáhirih the part of those who believed that the Bábí Faith was independent of Islám. When Ṭáhirih appeared unveiled in the assembled company, some believers were so shocked that they ran away from Badasht and did not return. One man tried to cut his own throat in horror at this violation of one of the practices of Islám. Ṭáhirih, unperturbed by the tumult she had aroused, and radiant with joyful certitude, proclaimed the advent of a new day. Those who remained firm in their new belief were greatly strengthened in their faith and enthusiasm. However, a few of the Bábís had, even before the conference of Badasht, abused the teachings of the Báb by treating their freedom from the traditional practices of Islám as an excuse for immoderate behaviour. They now took Ṭáhirih's unprecedented action in abandoning her veil as a signal for selfishness and anti-social behaviour. The excesses of these few misguided men aroused the hostility of the people living near Badasht and led to all the Bábís being physically attacked.

Immediately after the conference, as they moved away from Badasht, the Bábís were set upon by the inhabitants of a village called Níyálá. The attack came at dawn as they were all resting and it was so sudden and fierce that all the Bábís except for Bahá'u'lláh, Ṭáhirih and one young man, scattered to seek safety. After the first fierce rush was over, Bahá'u'lláh succeeded in pointing out to the villagers their wrong-doing and managed to recover some of the property that they had stolen.

The few Bábís who had brought the wrath of the people of

Níyálá onto their companions were so frightened by this attack that they immediately abandoned the faith of the Báb.

After the attack at Níyálá, the believers bade each other farewell and went their separate ways. Bahá'u'lláh went to His home in Núr in Mázindarán. Quddús and Ṭáhirih also went to Mázindarán and Quddús was arrested there. He was taken to the town of Ámul, the regional capital of the province where he was kept at the home of the leading divine of the town.

After being detained for a short while at the camp of Prince Ḥamzih Mírzá, Mullá Ḥusayn was able to return to Mashhad. He began preparations for a journey to Karbilá and many of his followers begged to be allowed to accompany him. While he was occupied in this way, a messenger arrived from Chihríq, bringing to Mullá Ḥusayn the Báb's own green turban, the sign of His descent from Muḥammad, and this message:

'Adorn your head with My green turban, the emblem of My lineage, and, with the Black Standard unfurled before you, hasten . . . and lend your assistance to My beloved Quddús.'

Mullá Ḥusayn obeyed instantly. He took his companions with him, and a short distance from Mashhad he gathered them about him, hoisted a black flag, placed the Báb's turban on his head and gave the signal for the march to Ámul to begin. There were two hundred and two Bábís with him. It was the twenty-first of July 1848. A thousand years earlier one of the followers of Muḥammad had recorded these words of the Prophet:

'Should your eyes behold the Black Standard proceeding from Khurásán, hasten ye towards them, even though ye should have to crawl over the snow, inasmuch as they proclaim the advent of the promised Mihdí, the Vicegerent of God.'

As they travelled towards Ámul, Mullá Ḥusayn and his

companions gave the message of the Báb to the people of all the towns and villages that they passed. They asked a few of those who responded to them in each place to join them on their march, but they met with such general hostility that they could not stay in any town or village. At Ní<u>sh</u>ápúr the owner of the richest turquoise mine in the area joined them, tossing on one side not only his wealth of precious gems but all the honour and prestige that his fellow citizens had heaped upon him, and rode towards Ámul with a joyful heart. Each one of the growing band of Bábís made a similar choice. Whether rich or poor, learned or illiterate, they knew only that the message they were hearing filled the deepest longing of their hearts and that they had to follow wherever it might lead them.

CHAPTER 30

TRIAL AT TABRÍZ

While these stirring events were taking place in Khurásán, the Grand Vizier issued orders for the Báb to be taken to Tabríz. His plan of isolating the Báb and thus destroying the Bábí movement had once again miscarried but he thought he could see a chance of using the situation to his advantage. Ḥájí Mírzá Áqásí badly wanted to gain favour with the orthodox Muslim clergy. The ill-health of the Sháh was a major factor in causing him to seek this favour and support.

Ḥájí Mírzá Áqásí announced that a convocation of clergy would be held in Tabríz to decide on a fitting punishment for the Báb and to devise a plan for eliminating the Bábí movement. Before the summons reached Chihríq, the Báb had already asked those Bábís who had come to the area to leave again and had arranged for all the writings that He had revealed in Máh-Kú and Chihríq to be moved to a safe place in Tabríz. The Báb was taken to Tabríz through Urúmíyyih rather than through Khuy where He had many followers. He reached Urúmíyyih on a Friday and was welcomed courteously by the Prince-governor of the city who decided to test the courage of the Báb. He knew that the Báb would visit the public bath and he offered to let the Báb ride a horse which he owned to the bath. The Prince knew that the horse was wild and dangerous and that no one had yet managed to control it. The Prince's groom tried to warn the Báb about the horse and advised Him not to ride it.

'Fear not,' said the Báb. 'Do as you have been bidden and commit Us to the care of the Almighty.'

The public square of Urúmíyyih was crowded, as the townspeople had been told of the Prince's plan and had come to see what would happen. The horse was brought to the Báb. He quietly approached it, took hold of the bridle and gently caressed it. The horse stood perfectly still while the Báb mounted and it carried Him meekly to the bath. A crowd of people rushed after Him trying to kiss His stirrups and had to be held back by the Prince's attendants. The Prince walked on foot beside the Báb all the way to the bath and later went to meet Him as He rode the same horse back again. The crowd rushed to carry away the water which the Báb had used.

The Báb reached Tabríz in the last week of July 1848, just as Mullá Ḥusayn and his companions were beginning their march towards Ámul. Tabríz was in turmoil and the authorities did not think that it was safe to lodge the Báb within the city walls. They made arrangements for Him to stay in a house a short distance outside the city. When He was brought into the city and led to the governor's residence where the convocation was to be held, crowds besieged the entrance to the hall and guards had to force a way through so that the Báb could enter the hall.

When He arrived inside the hall, there was only one seat in the crowded room still empty. This was the seat of honour which was being kept for the governor, the young Crown Prince, heir-apparent to his dying father. The Báb greeted the assembly and took the vacant seat. Majesty, dignity and power shone from His being. There was a deep, mysterious silence in the hall and no one dared say a word. Then one man, tutor to the Crown Prince, addressed the Báb:

'Whom do you claim to be', he asked, 'and what is the message which you have brought?'

The Báb replied:

'I am, I am, I am, the Promised One! I am the One whose

name you have for a thousand years invoked, at whose mention you have risen, whose advent you have longed to witness, and the hour of whose Revelation you have prayed God to hasten. Verily I say, it is incumbent upon the peoples of both the East and the West to obey My word and to pledge allegiance to My person.'

A feeling of awe seized all who were present. Heads bowed and faces grew pale. Then one white-bearded divine, who had once been a pupil of Siyyid Káẓim but who had caused his teacher to weep for his pupil's insincerity and perversity, began to scold the Báb.

'You wretched and immature lad of Shíráz! ' he began. 'You have already convulsed and subverted 'Iráq; do you now wish to arouse a like turmoil in Ádhirbáyján?'

'Your Honour,' the Báb replied, 'I have not come hither of My own accord, I have been summoned to this place.'

'Hold your peace,' the divine retorted, 'you perverse and contemptible follower of Satan!'

'Your Honour,' the Báb said, 'I maintain what I have already declared.'

Then the tutor of the Crown Prince began again.

'The claim which you have advanced', he said to the Báb, 'is a stupendous one; it must needs be supported by the most incontrovertible evidence.'

'The mightiest, the most convincing evidence of the truth of the Mission of the Prophet of God', the Báb replied, 'is admittedly His own Word. He Himself testifies to this truth: "Is it not enough for them that We have sent down to Thee the Book?" The power to produce such evidence has been given to Me by God. Within the space of two days and two nights, I declare Myself able to reveal verses of such number as will equal the whole of the Qur'án.'

The Prince's tutor then challenged the Báb to describe the proceedings of their gathering in language similar to that of the Qur'án. The Báb agreed to do this. He began:

'In the name of God, the Merciful, the Compassionate, praise be to Him who has created the heaven and the earth.'

At this point He was rudely interrupted by the same white-bearded divine who had first scolded Him. His complaint was that the Báb had ignored a minor rule of grammar.

'This self-appointed Qá'im of ours', he cried out haughtily, 'has at the very start of his address betrayed his ignorance of the most rudimentary rules of grammar!'

'The Qur'án itself', pleaded the Báb, 'does in no wise accord with the rules and conventions amongst men. The Word of God can never be subject to the limitations of His creatures . . .'

After further explaining this statement, the Báb repeated the same words and again the same divine interrupted, raising the same objection. Then another divine put to Him another trifling question about a point of grammar. The Báb replied with a verse from the Qur'án:

'Far be the glory of thy Lord, the Lord of all greatness, from what they impute to Him, and peace be upon His Apostles! And praise be to God, the Lord of the worlds.' He rose and left the meeting.

The Prince's tutor and a few of the divines were distressed at the course the meeting had taken and at the discourtesy which had been shown to the Báb. Others agitated for action against Him, playing on the fears of the majority that their own positions were threatened by the growth of His Cause. It was decided that the Báb be taken to the home of one of the chief religious leaders in Tabríz and be beaten by the governor's bodyguard. The guards refused to have anything to do with the matter, saying that it was solely a matter for the divines and nothing to do with them. The chief of the religious court of Tabríz, himself a siyyid, decided to beat the Báb himself. The Báb was taken to his home. The chief of the court struck Him eleven times with rods on the soles of His feet. One of the rods which was meant to strike His feet struck His face, causing a wound. The Báb was treated for His wounded face by an English doctor, a Dr Cormick, who has left this description of Him:

'He was very thankful for my attentions to him. He was a very mild and delicate-looking man, rather small in stature and very fair for a Persian, with a melodious soft voice . . . his whole look and deportment went far to dispose one in his favour. Of his doctrine I heard nothing from his own lips, although the idea was that there existed in his religion a certain approach to Christianity. He was seen by some Armenian carpenters, who were sent to make some repairs in his prison, reading the Bible, and he took no pains to conceal it, but on the contrary told them of it. Most assuredly the Musulmán fanaticism does not exist in his religion, as applied to Christians, nor is there that restraint of females that now exists.'

The chief of the court, who had beaten the Báb, was struck with paralysis soon afterwards and died an excruciatingly painful death in the same year.

The Báb was taken back to Chihríq at the beginning of August 1848. From the castle He wrote a letter to the Grand Vizier which is known as the Sermon of Wrath. He sent it to Ḥujjat who had it delivered to Hájí Mírzá Áqásí. By the time the Báb's letter reached him, the Grand Vizier's career was already over. He had left the imperial court out of fear for his own safety as the Sháh lay on his deathbed, and gone to the village of 'Abbásábád which he owned. There his bodyguard, recruited from the people of Máh-Kú, deserted him. He wrote to the Crown Prince and to a number of prominent courtiers pleading for friendship, but he received no replies. He tried to get back into Ṭihrán to his own residence but was turned away from the city. He set out for

Á<u>dh</u>irbáyján, planning to take refuge in Máh-Kú but was turned back when he had gone only a short distance and sought refuge in a holy shrine. On 4 September 1848 Muḥammad <u>Sh</u>áh died and a new ruler succeeded to the throne of Persia. Ḥájí Mírzá Áqásí's vast possessions were confiscated by the state. He managed to find refuge in Karbilá where he died the following year, sick, friendless and alone.

IX

An Ocean of Sorrow

September 1848 – June 1850

CHAPTER 31

THE SIEGE OF SHAYKH ṬABARSÍ

The new ruler of Persia, Náṣiri'd-Dín Sháh, was seventeen years old. His Grand Vizier was a man named Mírzá Taqí Khán. Mírzá Taqí Khán's father had been a cook in the household of the brilliant minister Qá'im Maqám, whose death Muḥammad Sháh had arranged at the start of his own reign. Qá'im Maqám had been the first to notice the remarkable ability of his cook's son. Mírzá Taqí Khán used this great ability to raise himself from his lowly origin to a position of power at court. He was known to be capable and very strong-willed and when the Crown Prince became the Sháh, Mírzá Ṭaqí Khán became, in all but name, the ruler of Persia.

After returning from Tabríz to Chihríq, the Báb was again able to communicate freely with His followers, for Yaḥyá Khán continued to be devoted to his prisoner and allowed the Bábí pilgrims to stay in Chihríq. One of those who came was Ḥájí Mírzá Siyyid 'Alí, the Báb's uncle. It was two years since Ḥájí Mírzá Siyyid 'Alí had seen his beloved Nephew and he could no longer bear the separation from Him. He settled his affairs in Shíráz and took the long road north to Ádhirbáyján. He stayed some time at Chihríq and his visit brought much happiness to the Báb. Ḥájí Mírzá Siyyid 'Alí left Chihríq with his own faith in the Báb greatly strengthened.

While the Báb received visitors at Chihríq, revealed tablets and continued to write the Persian Bayán, Mullá Ḥusayn and his companions, now nearing three hundred, continued on their journey towards Ámul where Quddús was held. Their march was peaceful and they had no intention of harming anyone. They wanted to demonstrate their faith in the Báb and their complete obedience to His command. They knew that they would sooner or later meet with opposition from those who felt threatened by their numbers. Mullá Ḥusayn repeatedly warned them of the dangers that lay ahead, saying, 'This is the way that leads to our Karbilá. Whoever is unprepared for the great trials that lie before us, let him now repair to his home and give up the journey.'

As Mullá Ḥusayn and his companions crossed the flat marshlands of Mázindarán and drew near to the town of Bárfurúsh, the birthplace of Quddús, the chief of the divines of that town roused the townspeople into a fury against them. The inhabitants of Bárfurúsh rushed out and attacked the Bábís, but the Bábís successfully repulsed their attack and the people of Bárfurúsh, seeing they could not defeat the Bábís, asked for a truce. The leading citizens of the town begged Mullá Ḥusayn to leave the area at once as his presence there was causing such agitation. The chief military officer in the province swore on the Qur'án that his soldiers would escort Mullá Ḥusayn and his companions safely away from the area. But the same divine who had incited the people to attack the Bábís persuaded the leader of the military escort, a man named Khusraw, to disobey his instructions. Khusraw took a route through the nearby forests, and once well into the forest ordered his men to attack and kill all the Bábís. The Bábís defended themselves ably and when the fight was over it was discovered that in the struggle Khusraw and all his men, except one, had been killed. Mullá Ḥusayn sent the sole survivor back to Bárfurúsh to tell the townspeople what had happened.

This attack and other raids by hostile villages forced Mullá Ḥusayn to seek a place of safety. Instructing his companions to leave behind them everything except their swords and their horses, Mullá Ḥusayn led them to the shrine of Shaykh Ṭabarsí which is about fourteen miles south-east of Bárfurúsh. They reached the shrine some time in October 1848. The Shaykh of Ṭabarsí had been one of those men who had transmitted the traditions of the Imáms to the people. Mullá Ḥusayn saw the shrine as a place of refuge in which he and his companions might live without being disturbed. He directed the Bábís to build defensive walls around the shrine and work began. They were continually harassed by local villagers as they built the walls and often had to stop work in order to defend themselves and beat off attacks.

As soon as the walls were complete, Bahá'u'lláh visited Shaykh Ṭabarsí and urged Mullá Ḥusayn to lose no time in seeking the release of Quddús. He recommended that a small group of men be sent to demand the release of Quddús. Bahá'u'lláh did not stay long at the fort but left for Núr and Ṭihrán. His advice was followed, a group of Bábís went to Ámul and their demand was met. Quddús arrived at Shaykh Ṭabarsí in December and was received with great joy and respect by all the Bábís. Bahá'u'lláh set out for Shaykh Ṭabarsí a second time, but this time He was stopped by the authorities and taken to Ámul where He was arrested and bastinadoed. He and His companions were sent back to Ṭihrán, and were thus unable to join the defenders of Shaykh Ṭabarsí.

The chief divine of Bárfurúsh, incensed by what had already happened and jealous of the power of attraction which the fort of Shaykh Ṭabarsí had for some of the local people, wrote a false account of the Bábís' activities to the new Sháh, encouraging the Sháh to destroy the fort and kill its defenders. He suggested that this action would be a fitting demonstration of power at the start of his new reign and would impress all his subjects. This idea appealed greatly to the new Grand Vizier, Mírzá Ṭaqí Khán. An army of twelve thousand was sent against the three hundred and thirteen defenders of Shaykh Ṭabarsí. The army surrounded the fort and a long siege began.

The Bábís were not soldiers. Most of them were craftsmen, labourers, small traders and students of theology and there were a few amongst them who had been respected divines. Yet they repulsed the attacks and scattered the army sent against them. To his fury, the Grand Vizier found that several professional armies were unable to capture the Bábís' fort. Several military commanders died on the field of battle as, time after time, a handful of Bábís rode out of Shaykh Ṭabarsí and scattered the Sháh's armies. The Bábís' food and water supplies were cut off and cannon were brought and used against them.

In January 1849 Mullá Ḥusayn was wounded as he led an attack and he died in the fort as a result of his wounds. Food was so scarce that the Bábís had to eat grass, the leaves of trees, the skin and ground bones of their slaughtered horses and even the boiled leather of their saddles. At one time they went for eighteen days with no food at all but the leather of their shoes. They held out against overwhelming odds until the end of April when they were defeated by treachery.

In April 1849, a prince, a brother of the Sháh, who was leading one of the armies, took a solemn oath on the Qur'án that the lives of the Bábís would be spared and their property would not be harmed if they gave themselves up peacefully. Quddús, although suspecting treachery, accepted the Prince's offer. He left the fort on a horse sent for him by the Prince and two hundred and two of the Bábís followed him on foot, while only a small group of their companions remained in the fort. Once most of the Bábís were out of the fort, the oath was forgotten. The Prince held the larger group captive and ordered his soldiers to attack the Bábís remaining in the fort. The defenders were killed, the fort razed to the ground and the bodies of many Bábís were mutilated and scattered through the forest. Only a few who were left for dead managed to crawl away from the place of slaughter.

The Prince then had all the captives brought before him. He found that three or four of them were very wealthy and he offered them their lives for a heavy ransom. He sold a few into slavery and ordered the soldiers to kill the rest, all but Quddús. Some Bábís were cut to pieces with swords, others were torn apart, some were tied to trees and riddled with bullets, others were burnt or fired from cannon. Quddús was taken to his home town of Bárfurúsh and handed over to the leading divine of the town. He was forced to endure agonising tortures and at the height of these torments was heard to cry out:

'Forgive, O my God, the trespasses of this people. Deal with them in Thy mercy, for they know not what we already have discovered and cherish.'

He was then led to the crowded square of the town where the chief divine himself took an axe and struck him down. The frenzied mob rushed at his fallen body with whatever weapons they had, hacked at it, tore it to pieces and burnt the shattered remains on a blazing fire. The charred remains of Quddús's body were left on the ground, but that night one compassionate divine of Bárfurúsh went there after all the rest had left, gathered up the few burnt fragments of Quddús's body and reverently buried them.

News of the massacre at Shaykh Ṭabarsí reached the Báb in June 1849. He was overwhelmed with grief. Nine of the Letters of the Living, His chosen disciples, died at Shaykh Ṭabarsí, including Mullá Ḥusayn, His beloved first disciple, and Quddús, youngest in years but foremost in rank. The

Báb's secretary recorded:

'The Báb was heart-broken . . . He was crushed with grief, a grief that stilled His voice and silenced His pen. For nine days He refused to meet any of His friends . . . Whatever meat or drink we offered Him, He was disinclined to touch. Tears rained continually from His eyes and expressions of anguish dripped unceasingly from His lips. I could hear Him, from behind the curtain, give vent to His feelings of sadness as He communed, in the privacy of His cell, with His Beloved. I attempted to jot down the effusions of His sorrow as they poured forth from His wounded heart. Suspecting that I was attempting to preserve the lamentations He uttered, He bade me destroy whatever I had recorded. Nothing remains of the moans and cries with which that heavy-laden heart sought to relieve itself of the pangs that had seized it. For a period of five months He languished, immersed in an ocean of despondency and sorrow.'

Some time in November 1849 the Báb began to write again. The first page that He wrote He dedicated to Mullá Ḥusayn and for a whole week He revealed tablets in praise of Quddús, Mullá Ḥusayn and their companions of Shaykh Ṭabarsí. In late November he sent a believer named Sayyáḥ to Mázindarán with these instructions:

'Arise, and with complete detachment proceed, in the guise of a traveller, to Mázindarán, and there visit, on My behalf, the spot which enshrines the bodies of those immortals who, with their blood, have sealed their faith in My Cause. As you approach the precincts of that hallowed ground, put off your shoes and, bowing your head in reverence to their memory, invoke their names and prayerfully make the circuit of their shrine. Bring back to Me, as a remembrance of your visit, a handful of that holy earth which covers the remains of My beloved ones, Quddús and Mullá

Ḥusayn. Strive to be back ere the day of Naw-Rúz, that you may celebrate with Me that festival, the only one I probably shall ever see again.'

Sayyáḥ carried out the Báb's instructions. On his way to Shaykh Ṭabarsí he passed through Ṭihrán and visited the house of Bahá'u'lláh. It was midwinter and very cold. Snow had fallen. Sayyáḥ travelled as a dervish, bare-footed and very poorly dressed. Vaḥíd was a guest of Bahá'u'lláh at the time. When he learnt that Sayyáḥ had come from the presence of the Báb Vaḥíd rushed forward, knelt down and reverently kissed the mud-covered feet of the traveller.

While Sayyáḥ stayed a short while in Tihrán, Bahá'u'lláh wrote a letter to the Báb and gave it to Sayyáḥ to carry back to Chihríq. In a reply to this letter, the Báb refers to Mírzá Yaḥyá, a young half-brother of Bahá'u'lláh. He commits Mírzá Yaḥyá to the care of Bahá'u'lláh and urges that attention be given to his education and training. The Báb had agreed with a plan put forward by Bahá'u'lláh and one other believer that Mírzá Yaḥyá be known as the appointed nominee of the Báb until such time as 'He Whom God shall make manifest' should appear. This was done to draw attention away from Bahá'u'lláh. Mírzá Yaḥyá spent much of his time in hiding or in disguise away from Ṭihrán and other major cities of Persia.

CHAPTER 32

THE SEVEN MARTYRS OF ṬIHRÁN

The episode of Shaykh Ṭabarsí had been a severe shock to the authorities and particularly to Mírzá Taqí Khán, the Grand Vizier. The length of time that the Bábís had held out, the large numbers of soldiers that they had defeated and the fact that they were only finally defeated by a trick made the Grand Vizier determined to wipe out the entire Bábí 'heresy' as soon as possible. Ṭihrán seethed with rumours as to what the Grand Vizier would do next.

Ḥájí Mírzá Siyyid 'Alí, the Báb's uncle, had recently reached Ṭihrán after visiting Chihríq. His friends urged him to leave. It was not safe to be a Bábí anywhere in Persia but it was particularly unsafe for prominent and respected citizens who were known to be Bábís to remain in the capital. In reply to the entreaties of his friends, Ḥájí Mírzá Siyyid 'Alí said:

'Why fear for my safety? Would that I too could share in the banquet which the hand of Providence is spreading for His chosen ones!'

One man who had attended some meetings of the Bábís gave the names of fifty of the believers in Ṭihrán to the authorities and a story was circulated, which was not generally believed, that these fifty people were involved in a plot to kill the Grand Vizier. Orders went out that all fifty be seized immediately, but only fourteen of them could be found and these were arrested. Ḥájí Mírzá Siyyid 'Alí was amongst them. During mid-February of 1850 all fourteen were confined in the house of the Kalántar, the mayor of Ṭihrán. Ṭáhirih was also under arrest at this time and was kept confined in a room on the upper floor of the same house. The fourteen men were ill-treated and tortured in order to make them give the names of other Bábís to the authorities.

The torture, the continual ill-treatment and the cruel ingenuity of their captors who used all the means of pressure that they could devise in order to obtain the information they wanted, brought no result. The matter was then referred to the Grand Vizier who announced that they would all be executed unless they recanted their belief in the Báb. The Sháh himself did not take an active part in what was done to the Bábís but simply left it to his Grand Vizier to do what he thought best. Mírzá Taqí Khán was so powerful that no one dared to question or disapprove of his decisions. Under pressure and torture, seven of the Bábís recanted their faith and were immediately released. The remaining seven, including Ḥájí Mírzá Siyyid 'Alí, refused.

All of the seven remaining Bábí prisoners were well-respected citizens of outstanding ability and character. Two of them were wealthy merchants, one was a divine noted for his piety and one had been a famous dervish. They had many influential friends who first tried to persuade them to recant their faith and then, seeing that this would not be successful, tried other means of rescuing them. A number of rich merchants tried to pay a ransom for the life of Ḥájí Mírzá Siyyid 'Alí. The Grand Vizier told him that just one word of recantation would set him free and pledged that, if he would only recant, he could spend the remaining days of his life with honour and dignity. Ḥájí Mírzá Siyyid 'Alí responded:

'To refuse to acknowledge the Mission of the Siyyid-i-Báb would be to apostatise from the Faith of my forefathers and to deny the Divine character of the Message which Muḥammad, Jesus, Moses, and all the Prophets of the past have revealed . . . I only request of you that you allow me to be the first to lay down my life in the path of my beloved Kinsman.'

A great crowd gathered in the public square of Ṭihrán to see the executions carried out. As Ḥájí Mírzá Siyyid 'Alí was led to the place of execution, he was heard to be praising God for having granted all that he desired.

'Hear me, O people,' he cried to the crowds that pressed around him. 'I have offered myself up as a willing sacrifice in the path of the Cause of God . . . For over a thousand years, you have prayed and prayed again that the promised Qá'im be made manifest. At the mention of His name, how often have you cried, from the depths of your hearts: "Hasten, O God, His coming; remove every barrier that stands in the way of His appearance!" And now that He is come, you have driven Him to a hopeless exile in a remote and sequestered corner of Ádhirbáyján and have risen to exterminate His companions. Were I to invoke the malediction of God upon you, I am certain that His avenging wrath would grievously afflict you. Such is not, however, my prayer. With my last breath, I pray that the Almighty may wipe away the stain of your guilt and enable you to awaken from the sleep of heedlessness.'

Ḥájí Mírzá Siyyid 'Alí was then executed. Many people were greatly moved by the words he had spoken just before his death. The executioner was so shaken that he left, pretending that the sword which he had just used needed to be re-sharpened and he did not return. Another executioner was brought forward to continue the task.

The remaining six Bábís were all eager to die. Their defiant statements, their ecstatic joy, their forgiveness of those who persecuted them and their eloquent appeals and challenges shook the hearts of all who watched them die and of all who heard of their martyrdom. Their bodies were left where they had fallen for three days and three nights, during which time thousands of the citizens of Ṭihrán kicked them, pelted them with stones, spat on their faces, heaped refuse over them, mocked at them and cursed them.

The Báb, already overwhelmed by the calamity of Shaykh Ṭabarsí, wept for them in his desolate prison and revealed a tablet in their honour in which he referred to them as the 'Seven Goats' spoken of in the traditions of Islám, who on the Day of Judgement shall 'walk in front of the promised Qá'im'. The Seven Martyrs of Ṭihrán were buried together in one grave outside the city gate. While the Báb reeled from this further heavy blow, another siege was already under way – at Nayríz – the home town of Vaḥíd.

CHAPTER 33

NAYRÍZ AND ZANJÁN

From the moment that he had accepted the message of the Báb. Vaḥíd had travelled and taught tirelessly. In the early days of the siege of Shaykh Ṭabarsí he had been in Burújird and Kurdistán. As soon as he learnt that Mullá Ḥusayn was going to rescue Quddús, he prepared to join him. He hurried to Ṭihrán to prepare for the next stage of the journey. Bahá'u'lláh arrived back in Ṭihrán while Vaḥíd was there and advised Vaḥíd that it would not now be possible for him to join the other besieged Bábís. Vaḥíd was saddened by this and spent much time with Bahá'u'lláh increasing his knowledge of the Cause of the Báb and his devotion to it. From Ṭihrán he went to teach at Qum, Káshán, Iṣfáhán, Ardistán and Ardikán. Wherever he went he taught fearlessly and attracted many souls to the message of the Báb.

In January of 1850 he reached Yazd where he owned a beautiful mansion. Vaḥíd was a very wealthy man. His wife and four sons lived in this house in Yazd, he had another large house in Dáráb, his ancestral home, and a third, sumptuously furnished, in Nayríz. The leading divines and notables of Yazd received Vaḥíd courteously. He taught in Yazd as he had elsewhere, with great enthusiasm and without fear for his own safety.

As news of Vaḥíd's activities spread through the surrounding district, more and more people came to Yazd to hear him. Some believed but others began to oppose him fiercely. His house was attacked both by a mob and a regiment of soldiers. The unwise actions of one Bábí, who refused to follow Vaḥíd's advice and insisted on retaliating against the attackers, increased the danger greatly. Vaḥíd told his followers to leave Yazd quickly and quietly. He arranged for his wife to take two of their sons to her father's house and he prepared to abandon his beautiful home.

'This palatial residence', Vaḥíd told his wife, 'I have built with the sole intention that it should be eventually demolished in the path of the Cause, and the stately furnishings with which I have adorned it have been purchased in the hope that one day I shall be able to sacrifice them for the sake of my Beloved.'

Vaḥíd left Yazd at night with his two young sons and two companions. They hid in nearby hills while soldiers from Yazd searched for them and then made their way to the south on foot through the Zagros mountains towards Nayríz. In Yazd Vaḥíd's house was first plundered and then completely demolished. Vaḥíd taught in every village that he passed through. Where people responded to his message, he stayed for one night in order to increase their knowledge and where no one responded at all, he did not stay.

As he approached Nayríz, the entire population of the quarter where his house stood came out to welcome him. The governor of Nayríz threatened everyone who went to see him with the loss of their possessions and even their lives but it made no difference. The governor became so frightened that Vaḥíd's followers might attack him that he moved out of Nayríz to a village where there was a large fortress. Vaḥíd went directly to the mosque when he entered Nayríz and addressed the people:

'My sole purpose', he told them, 'in coming to Nayríz is to proclaim the Cause of God. I thank and glorify Him for having enabled me to touch your hearts with His message. No need for me to tarry any longer in your midst, for if I prolong my stay, I fear that the governor will ill-treat you because of me.'

But the people he addressed would not allow him to leave at once. He agreed to stay with them for a few days and every day more people were attracted to his teaching. The governor raised an army of about a thousand men, both cavalry and infantry, and planned to seize Vaḥíd in a sudden attack. News of this was brought to Vaḥíd. He advised about twenty of his companions, who had reached Nayríz with him, to occupy the fort of Kh͟ájih which stood in the town and to reinforce its barricades. The governor occupied a fort in a neighbouring quarter and launched an attack on the fort of Kh͟ájih. As soon as he heard of the first attack, Vaḥíd joined the other Bábís inside the fort. There were seventy-two Bábís there when the siege began. They easily repulsed the first attacks and the governor sent to S͟hīráz for reinforcements. As at S͟hayk͟h Ṭabarsí, the stage was set for a long siege.

At Zanján, the home town of Ḥujjat, the Bábís were also in great difficulties. In May of 1850 the largest and fiercest of the attacks launched at the Bábís began. Ḥujjat, that independent-minded and outspoken follower of the Báb, had enjoyed some protection under the regime of Muḥammad S͟háh but he had none under the new regime. The divines of Zanján hated him and longed to destroy him. He had been kept under house arrest for some time in Ṭihrán but in 1850 he was back in his home town.

A minor quarrel between children, in which Ḥujjat intervened to rescue a Bábí child, was the spark that set off the conflict. The divines tried to bring Ḥujjat before the governor but failed. Then they seized one of his companions, tortured and killed him. Then the governor decreed that everyone in Zanján should choose whose side they were on, the side of the Bábís or the divines, and the town was split into two opposing groups. Though hated by the authorities, Ḥujjat had a large following amongst the townspeople. Over three thousand of them sought refuge with him in a fort and the government forces again began to attack and besiege the Bábís.

News of the conflicts at Nayríz and Zanján reached the Báb in Chihríq and added greatly to His grief. He sent His writings, His pen-case, His seals and rings to Bahá'u'lláh together with a scroll of blue paper on which He had written, in the form of a pentacle, in the most exquisite handwriting, five hundred derivatives of the word Bahá.

The army sent against Vaḥíd and his companions at Nayríz was defeated with heavy losses. The end came at Nayríz, as at Shaykh Ṭabarsí, only through treachery. The military leaders sent a letter to Vaḥíd asking him to come out and explain his teachings to them. They promised, on the Qur'án, to investigate the Cause of the Báb sincerely. If they found it to be true, they would accept it, they said; if not, they would give Vaḥíd a safe conduct back to the fort and would resume the conflict.

Vaḥíd and five of his companions walked out of the fort to the army camp. For three days they were entertained lavishly, then the authorities forced Vaḥíd to write a letter to the rest of the besieged Bábís assuring them that a settlement had been reached. He tried to send a second letter informing them of the true facts but this letter did not get through to the fort.

The Bábís came out of the fort. The oaths and promises were forgotten. They were seized, chained, tortured with appalling cruelty and then killed. Their heads were stuffed with straw and carried on lances to Shíráz. Their wives and children were seized, abominably treated and taken to Shíráz. The fort was razed to the ground and many houses in Nayríz were destroyed. The entire quarter where Vaḥíd's house had stood was sacked and large sums of money were extorted from its inhabitants.

Vaḥíd was tied to a horse by his green turban, the emblem of his descent from Muḥammad. He was dragged through the streets of Nayríz, stoned and beaten to death and his body was trampled into the dust.

The Grand Vizier was badly shaken and seriously alarmed by the events of Nayríz. He believed that the interests of the state were in danger and that the government could not tolerate any more such upheavals. He raged that his predecessor, Ḥájí Mírzá Áqásí, had allowed the Bábí movement to get so out of hand. The Grand Vizier would have liked to have ruined the cause of the Báb by seeing the Báb defeated in argument by the divines but he did not dare to attempt this. Hearing the reports of his spies, he decided it was too great a risk to take. Instead, he decided that the Bábí movement must be completely destroyed and at once. Mírzá Taqí Khán gave orders that the Báb again be brought to Tabríz.

X

Tabríz

July 1850

CHAPTER 34

ANÍS, THE BÁB'S CHOSEN COMPANION

The Governor-General of Ádhirbáyján saw that the Grand Vizier's order was carried out. The Báb was treated with respect and consideration on the journey, was housed as a guest in the home of a friend of the Governor-General in Tabríz and was treated courteously. Three days later the Governor-General received a further order from Ṭihrán. It was brought to him by the Grand Vizier's own brother, Mírzá Ḥasan Khán. The Grand Vizier commanded the Governor-General to have the Báb executed in public on the very day that the order reached him. He also commanded that anyone who claimed to be a follower of the Báb should also be executed.

The Governor-General was amazed at this order and protested:

'The Amír', he said, 'would do better to entrust me with services of greater merit than the one with which he has now commissioned me . . . I am neither Ibn-i-Zíyád nor Ibn-i-Sa'd[1] that he should call upon me to slay an innocent descendant of the Prophet of God.'

Mírzá Ḥasan Khán reported this to the Grand Vizier who responded by ordering his brother to carry out the instructions himself and at once. He urged that it be done quickly before the month of Ramaḍán, the time of the Muslim fast, began. Mírzá Ḥasan Khán tried to inform the Governor-General of this new instruction but he could not do so for the

1. Persecutors of the descendants of Muḥammad.

Governor-General said that he was ill and unable to receive visitors.

Mírzá Ḥasan Khán gave orders that the Báb and Siyyid Ḥusayn be moved immediately from the house in which they were lodged to the city barracks. The Báb was stripped of His turban and His sash, the emblems of His descent from Muḥammad, and was led on foot to the citadel where the barracks were situated. The city was in turmoil as crowds of people filled the streets trying to get a glimpse of the Báb as He was taken to the citadel.

As the two prisoners, guarded by soldiers, approached the citadel of Tabríz, a young man pushed his way through the dense crowds with frantic haste and threw himself at the feet of the Báb. His face was haggard, his hair was unkempt and his feet were bare. He clutched at the hem of the Báb's clothes and begged:

'Send me not from Thee, O Master. Wherever Thou goest, suffer me to follow Thee.'

'Muḥammad-'Alí,' the Báb answered him, 'arise, and rest assured that you will be with Me. Tomorrow you shall witness what God has decreed.'

Two other followers of the Báb, moved by the action of the youth, also rushed forward to confess their loyalty to the Báb. These three were put into one cell at the barracks with the Báb and Siyyid Ḥusayn, His secretary. The Báb gave the name of Anís, which means 'Companion', to Muḥammad-'Alí.

Anís had for some time been a devoted follower of the Báb. He had longed to go to Chihríq but his father, who was a notable or leading citizen of Tabríz, objected so strongly to his son's belief that he locked him up in his own house, even though Anís was an adult, was married and had a young child. Anís had been locked up throughout the Báb's previous visit to Tabríz, but this treatment had not made him give up his belief in the Báb. He protested and complained of his father's behaviour and spent his days in a state of hopeless grief and longing. His father thought that his son had gone out of his mind and did not know what to do about it.

The family of Anís were related to Shaykh Ḥasan-i-Zunúzí, who had been the first Bábí pilgrim to reach Máh-Kú. Anís's father asked Shaykh Ḥasan to visit his son and try to calm him down. Shaykh Ḥasan visited Anís several times and found him tearful and miserable in his captivity. Then one day, when the Báb had been taken back to Chihríq after being beaten in Tabríz, Shaykh Ḥasan found his young relative transformed. His eyes were bright, his face was joyful and he was peaceful and calm. Shaykh Ḥasan recounted:

'His handsome face was wreathed in smiles as he stepped forward to receive me. "The eyes of my Beloved", he said as he embraced me, "have beheld this face, and these eyes have gazed upon His countenance. Let me tell you the secret of my happiness. After the Báb had been taken back to Chihríq one day, as I lay confined in my cell, I turned my heart to Him and besought Him in these words: 'Thou beholdest, O my Best-Beloved, my captivity and helplessness, and knowest how eagerly I yearn to look upon Thy face. Dispel the gloom that oppresses my heart, with the light of Thy countenance.' What tears of agonising pain I shed that hour! I was so overcome with emotion that I seemed to have lost consciousness. Suddenly I heard the voice of the Báb, and, lo! He was calling me. He bade me arise. I beheld the majesty of His countenance as He appeared before me. He smiled as He looked into my eyes. I rushed forward and flung myself at His feet. 'Rejoice,' He said; 'the hour is approaching when, in this very city, I shall be suspended before the eyes of the multitude and shall fall a victim to the fire of the enemy. I shall choose no one except you to share with Me the cup of martyrdom. Rest assured that this promise which I give you shall be fulfilled.' I was entranced by the beauty of that vision. When I recovered, I found myself immersed in an ocean of joy, a joy the radiance of which all the sorrows of the world could never obscure. That voice keeps ringing in my ears. That vision haunts me both in the daytime and in the night-season. The memory of that ineffable smile has dissipated the loneliness of my confinement. I am firmly convinced that the hour at which His pledge is to be fulfilled can no longer be delayed."'

Shaykh Ḥasan encouraged Anís to keep his vision a secret and to be very patient with his father. He persuaded the father to release his son from confinement, and from that moment on Anís lived in a state of great joy and contentment until the day that he heard the Báb was being taken to the barracks and rushed through the streets to Him.

CHAPTER 35
DARK NOON

The Báb knew that He would die the next day and on the night before His death He was full of joy. His last months at Chihríq had been laden with sorrows but this great grief suddenly lifted from Him. His face glowed with a joy that His companions had never seen before. He spoke cheerfully to comfort and encourage them.

'Tomorrow', He said, 'will be the day of My martyrdom. Would that one of you might now arise and, with his own hands, end My life. I prefer to be slain by the hand of a friend rather than by that of the enemy.' His companions wept on hearing these words and all refused, except for Anís who sprang forward and said that he would do whatever the Báb asked. The others were horrified and made him give up the idea at once, but when all was calm again the Báb said:

'This same youth who has risen to comply with My wish will, together with Me, suffer martyrdom. Him will I choose to share with Me its crown.'

Early the next morning, Mírzá Ḥasan Khán gave orders that the Báb be taken to the homes of the leading divines of Tabríz in order to obtain their written consent to His execution. The chief attendant arrived at the barracks while the Báb was giving some important instructions to Siyyid Ḥusayn. Siyyid Ḥusayn asked Him what he should do; should he acknowledge his belief in the Báb or conceal it.

'Confess not your faith,' the Báb advised him. 'Thereby you will be enabled, when your hour comes, to convey to those who are destined to hear you, the things of which you alone are aware.'

He was still speaking with Siyyid Ḥusayn when the chief attendant entered the room, interrupted the conversation and scolded the Báb for delaying their departure. The Báb responded with these words:

'Not until I have said to him all those things that I wish to say can any earthly power silence Me. Though all the world be armed against Me, yet shall they be powerless to deter Me from fulfilling, to the last word, My intention.'

The chief attendant was startled by this forthright speech but he quickly led the Báb away from the room, leaving Siyyid Ḥusayn locked inside it. The attendant put iron collars around the necks of the Báb and Anís and iron manacles on their wrists. A long cord was tied to each collar and by these they were led through the streets and markets of the city. In the crowded, narrow streets people climbed on each other's shoulders to get a better glimpse of the prisoners and hurl refuse and insults at them.

The divines already had the death warrants signed and sealed and did not even wish to see the Báb. When Anís was brought before them, they tried hard to make him recant his faith.

'Never will I renounce my Master,' Anís told them. 'He is the essence of my faith, and the object of my truest adoration. In Him I have found my paradise, and in the observance of His law I recognise the ark of my salvation.' One of the divines ordered him to be silent as his words showed that he was obviously out of his mind.

'I am not mad,' Anís retorted. 'Such a charge should rather be brought against you who have sentenced to death a man no less holy than the promised Qá'im. He is not a fool who has embraced His Faith and is longing to shed His blood in His path.'

They brought Anís's young child to him in order to weaken his resolve but he remained unshaken and committed the infant to God's care.

When they returned to the barracks square, the Báb was handed over to the care of Sám Khán, colonel of the Armenian regiment ordered to carry out the execution. Anís was taken back to the room where Siyyid Ḥusayn was still kept but he wept and begged to be allowed to remain with the Báb. He was then also handed over to Sám Khán with the orders that he too would be executed if he did not recant his faith.

Sám Khán was ill at ease. He was moved by what he had heard and seen of the Báb and was afraid that the execution might bring the wrath of God on him. He went to the Báb and said:

'I profess the Christian Faith and entertain no ill will against you. If your Cause be the Cause of Truth, enable me to free myself from the obligation to shed your blood.'

The Báb calmed him with these words:

'Follow your instructions, and if your intention be sincere, the Almighty is surely able to relieve you from your perplexity.'

Sám Khán went on carrying out his orders unhappily. The Báb and Anís were tied together with ropes and were hung onto a rope suspended from a nail driven into the wall. Anís asked that his own head might rest across the breast of the Báb so that he might shield Him from the full force of the bullets. The seven hundred and fifty soldiers of Sám Khán's regiment took up their positions in three lines, one line behind the other. A great crowd of the citizens of Tabríz had come to see the execution carried out and the roofs of all the surrounding buildings were crammed with people.

The soldiers took aim and fired, one row at a time. The noise was deafening and the square filled with the dense smoke of rifle fire. When the smoke began to lift, the astonished multitude saw Anís standing upright, smiling and unconcerned, his white tunic untouched by the thick smoke. The bullets had only severed the ropes which had bound him to the wall. There was no sign of the Báb.

Uproar broke out. Officials began to run to and fro shouting at each other and searching frantically for the Báb. The chief attendant who had interrupted His conversation earlier that morning found Him, in the locked room that He had occupied the night before, finishing that same conversation with Siyyid Ḥusayn. There was no sign on His body or His clothes that any one of the seven hundred and fifty bullets had gone near Him. He calmly finished what He had to say to Siyyid Ḥusayn. Then He turned to the bewildered and frightened chief attendant and said:

'I have finished My conversation with Siyyid Ḥusayn. Now you may proceed to fulfil your intention.' The man was so terrified that he left the barracks square at that moment and resigned his post. Sám Khán ordered his men out of the barracks yard and adamantly refused to have any more to do with anything that would bring harm to the Báb, even though he might himself be threatened with death.

Another regiment had to be brought in. It was a Náṣirí regiment, the same one that had guarded the Báb on His first enforced visit to Tabríz. The Báb and Anís were again tied up against the wall. The soldiers again took their places in three lines. This time the Báb addressed the crowds with these words:

'Had you believed in Me, O wayward generation,' He said, 'every one of you would have followed the example of this youth, who stood in rank above most of you, and willingly would have sacrificed himself in My path. The day will come when you will have recognised Me; that day I shall have ceased to be with you.'

As the shots were fired, a great wind arose and swept over the city. A whirlwind of dust came with it, a dust so dense that it hid the light of the sun and blinded the eyes of the people. A violent storm broke over their heads and the strange darkness lasted from noon until nightfall. The bodies of the Báb and Anís were shattered by the seven hundred and fifty bullets to such an extent that their flesh was blended together and could not be separated. The face of the Báb had not been marked by a single bullet; it was calm and serene.

EPILOGUE

At nightfall the bodies of the Báb and Anís were dragged through the streets of Tabríz and thrown out on the edge of the moat that surrounded the city. There is a tradition in Islám which states that the human remains of a Messenger of God will never be eaten by wild animals. The divines intended that wild dogs should consume the bodily remains of the Báb so that the people's faith in Him would be destroyed. Four companies of soldiers, each consisting of ten sentinels, were posted to keep watch and to prevent any Bábís from attempting to retrieve the bodies for decent burial.

Late the next day a Bábí named Ḥájí Sulaymán Khán arrived in Tabríz. He was a prominent figure in Persia and had intended to rescue the Báb from His impending execution. Hearing that he had come too late, Ḥájí Sulaymán Khán went straight to the mayor of Tabríz who was a personal friend of his. He told the mayor that he planned to make a surprise attack on the soldiers and carry away the bodies but the mayor told Ḥájí Sulaymán Khán that he had a better plan. He contacted a certain man named Ḥájí Alláh-Yár who had carried out a number of unusual commissions for him.

Ḥájí Alláh-Yár disguised himself as a madman and rescued the remains of the two bodies from the edge of the moat as the soldiers were keeping a careless watch. In the morning the soldiers reported that the remains of the bodies had been eaten by wild animals. Ḥájí Alláh-Yár refused to accept payment for what he had done and delivered the remains of the bodies to Sulaymán Khán who had them moved to a silk factory owned by a Bábí in the town of Mílán. On the third day after the execution they were sealed inside a casket and taken to a safe hiding-place.

Bahá'u'lláh directed the Bábís to transfer the casket secretly to Ṭihrán. It was kept hidden in several places in and around the city for almost fifty years. In 1898 'Abdu'l-Bahá, Bahá'u'lláh's son and His chosen successor, instructed the Bahá'ís to take the casket to the Holy Land and it was carried secretly through Iṣfáhán, Kirmánsháh, Baghdád and Damascus to Beirut. It was then taken by ship to 'Akká and reached the prison-city on 31 January 1899.

In 1890, just two years before His ascension, Bahá'u'lláh had shown 'Abdu'l-Bahá the exact spot on Mount Carmel where the remains of the Báb and Anís should be buried. It was a rocky hillside on the central slope of the mountain which rises above the bay of Haifa. It was ten years before 'Abdu'l-Bahá was able to begin to carry out the instructions of Bahá'u'lláh. During those years the casket was kept hidden in 'Akká while 'Abdu'l-Bahá managed, with very great difficulty, to obtain the land on Mount Carmel and build a road to the site. When the foundations were laid for the building, He was once again, as a result of the activities of the Covenant-breakers, imprisoned in 'Akká. During His imprisonment work at the site continued and a simple stone building was erected to receive the casket. In 1908 'Abdu'l-Bahá was released from prison and on 21 March 1909 He Himself laid the precious casket within a marble sarcophagus in a vault beneath the building.

Forty years and two world wars later, Shoghi Effendi, the great-grandson of Bahá'u'lláh and the Guardian of the Bahá'i Faith, began to direct the building of a fitting superstructure for the Shrine of the Báb. Bahá'ís from all around the world contributed funds for the building of the white marble superstructure which was completed in 1953.

The Shrine of the Báb is now a place of light and purity, of strength and breath-taking beauty. It is capped with a golden dome and stands in a beautiful garden overlooking the bay and facing towards 'Akká and Bahjí. In the daytime sunlight gleams on the gold-tiled roof which can be seen far out at sea and at night the shrine glows like a jewel with light from the eighteen tall windows, one for each of the Letters of the Living.

Bahá'ís from all around the world come in increasing numbers to the shrine to pray and to give thanks for the life of the Báb, Who gave His own life to proclaim the coming of Bahá'u'lláh.

* * * * *

It is now more than one hundred and forty years since the Báb declared His mission. During that time thousands of His countrymen and women have joyfully accepted torture and death rather than deny their faith in Him. The house in Shíráz where the Báb declared His mission has been razed to the ground in a deliberate attempt to put out the light that He brought into the world. But the light of the Báb's message has gone around the planet and burns more brightly with each passing year. Men and women on every continent and island are hearing of the message of the Báb and Bahá'u'lláh and are finding in Their teachings refreshment for their souls, the renewal of their highest ideals and aspirations and a joyous confidence in the certainty of a peaceful and happy future for the human family.

A NOTE ON SOURCES

This account of the life of the Báb is based, in large part, on *The Dawn-Breakers: Nabíl's Narrative of the Early Days of the Bahá'í Revelation*, by Nabíl-i-A'ẓam, and on two titles by H. M. Balyuzi, *The Báb, the Herald of the Day of Days* and *Khadíjih Bagum, the Wife of the Báb*. Certain quotations are taken from *A Traveler's Narrative written to illustrate the episode of the Báb* by 'Abdu'l-Bahá and *God Passes By* by Shoghi Effendi. Some words of the Báb are quoted from *Selections from the Writings of the Báb*.

The author's intent has been to provide a clear and straightforward historical account of the life of the Báb. It is her hope that, once this is obtained, her readers will be able to turn with confidence and enthusiasm to the titles listed above.

For those who wish to refer to exact quotations – for example, words spoken by the Báb and various other people – and to the episodes surrounding them, page references are listed below.

SELECTIONS FROM THE WRITINGS OF THE BÁB compiled by the Research Department of the Universal House of Justice and translated by Habíb Taherzadeh with the assistance of a committee at the Bahá'í World Centre. (Haifa: Bahá'í World Centre, 1976.)

Story page	*Source page*
33	41
34–5	59, 52, 53, 54, 56, 62

Story page	*Source page*
91	217
136	7
136–7	107–8
137	92, 98, 7

A TRAVELER'S NARRATIVE WRITTEN TO ILLUSTRATE THE EPISODE OF THE BÁB by 'Abdu'l-Bahá. Translated by E. G. Browne. (Wilmette: Bahá'í Publishing Trust, rev. edn 1980.)

Story page	*Source page*
119–20	11–12

GOD PASSES BY by Shoghi Effendi. (Wilmette: Bahá'í Publishing Trust, 1944.)

Story page	*Source page*
137	29–30
138	25

THE DAWN-BREAKERS: NABÍL'S NARRATIVE OF THE EARLY DAYS OF THE BAHÁ'Í REVELATION translated from the original Persian and edited by Shoghi Effendi. (Wilmette: Bahá'í Publishing Trust, 1932. London, Bahá'í Publishing Trust, 1953. Page numbers given here are from the US edition.)

Story page	*Source page*	*Story page*	*Source page*
5	5	11	40–41, 48
6	10	16	75–6
7	14	20	30,26
8	16	21	27
9	17, 8	22	27–8
10	25	23	253

Story page	*Source page*
25	77
29	53
30	55, 56
31	57
32–3	59–60
34	61
35	63
36	63
36–7	65
41	66
42	67–8
43	69
44	69–70
45	85–6
46	86–7, 123
46–7	92–4
48–9	90
51	96, 123
52	103
53–5	104–7
61	132
63	142
64	145
66–8	146–8
69–70	148–50
75–6	153
79	158
84	172
85–8	173–7
90	179
91	192
92–3	194–5
94–5	197–8
101	202
103	202, 204
104	205
105	209
107–9	212–214
113	215
114	218, 219
115	224
118	228
121	235, 236
122–3	236
124–5	238
125–6	240–41, 243
129	258
132–3	247–8
135	249
139	255
140–42	256–60
148	305
151	263
152	269
153	289
156	324, 351
158	309
159–61	315–19
168	326
171	411
172–3	430, 431
174	442
175–6	447–8
179	473, 479
185	506
186	507

Story page	*Source page*	*Story page*	*Source page*
187–8	307–8	191	512
189–90	508–10	192	513, 515

THE BÁB: THE HERALD OF THE DAY OF DAYS by H. M. Balyuzi. (Oxford: George Ronald, 1973.)

Story page	*Source page*
17	36
49	61
62	71
70	88
76–8	97–9
83	11–12
162	146–7

<u>KH</u>ADÍJIH BAGUM: THE WIFE OF THE BÁB by H. M. Balyuzi. (Oxford: George Ronald, 1981.)

Story page	*Source page*
24	8–9
62–3	36

LIST OF NAMES

Names are given in the form most frequently used in this book, in alphabetical order.

Aḥmad	the only child born to the Báb and Khadíjih-Bagum. He died in infancy in 1843
'Alí-Muḥammad, the Báb	The Qá'im, the Promised One. He was born in Shíráz in 1819, declared His mission in 1844 and was martyred in Tabríz on 9 July 1850
'Alí Khán	the Kurdish governor of the fortress of Máh-Kú who became devoted to the Báb and disobeyed the government's orders for the Báb's confinement
Anís	Mírzá Muḥammad-'Alíy-i-Zunúzí, a young Bábí of Tabríz who begged to be killed with the Báb. The Báb granted his request and named him 'Anís' which means 'Companion'
Bahá'u'lláh	Mirzá Ḥusayn-'Alí, a follower of the Báb, adopted the title 'Bahá'u'lláh' (The Glory of God) at the Conference of Badasht in 1848. The title 'Bahá'u'lláh' is first mentioned in the most important work of the Báb, the Bayán
Dr Cormick	An English doctor working in Tabríz who was called to treat the Báb after He was bastinadoed

Crown Prince ‘Abbás Mírzá — an heir-apparent to Fatḥ-‘Alí Sháh. He tried to bring about some reforms in Persia. He died a year before his father in 1833

Crown Prince Muḥammad-‘Alí Mírzá — Governor of Kirmansháh province and an heir to the Persian Throne. He died before his father, Fatḥ-‘Alí Sháh

Fatḥ-‘Alí Sháh — the third Qájár ruler of Persia (1797–1834)

Gurgín Khán — a nephew of Manúchihr Khán and his heir. He reported to the Sháh that his uncle had concealed the Báb in his home

Ḥájí ‘Alí-Askar — a Bábí of Tabríz who had failed to see the Báb in Shíráz but who visited Him seven times in Tabríz

Ḥájí Alláh-Yár — a citizen of Tabríz, a confidant of the mayor, and who rescued the bodies of the Báb and Anís

Ḥájí Mírzá ‘Alí — the father of Khadíjih-Bagum, the wife of the Báb

Ḥájí Mírzá Áqásí — Grand Vizier to Muḥammad Sháh. He had been the Sháh’s religious tutor. He fell from power in 1848 and died in 1849

Ḥájí Mírzá Jání — a prominent merchant of Káshán who became a Bábí

Ḥájí Mírzá Siyyid ‘Alí — a maternal uncle of the Báb who took care of the Báb when He was young. He became a devoted Bábí and was martyred in Ṭihrán in 1850

Ḥájí Mullá Taqíy-i-Baraqání — the uncle and father-in-law of Ṭáhirih. Murdered in Qazvín

Ḥájí Sulaymán Khán — a prominent Bábí who arranged for the rescue of the remains of the bodies of

	the Báb and Anís
Ḥasan	the servant of Mullá Ḥusayn who was arrested in Mashhad
Hashím	the name of the tribe into which the Prophet Muḥammad was born. The Báb, being a descendant of Muḥammad, was of the family of Hashím
Ḥujjat	Mullá Muḥammad-'Alí, a learned and outspoken religious leader of Zanján who became a Bábí. The Báb gave him the name 'Ḥujjat' which means 'The Proof'. Ḥujjat was martyred in Zanján in 1850
Ḥusayn Khán	the stern governor of Fárs province. He placed the Báb under house arrest and tried to kill him
Khadíjih-Bagum	the wife of the Báb. She believed in Him and lived until 1882
Khusraw	a military leader ordered to escort Mullá Ḥusayn and his companions safely away from Bárfurúsh
Manúchihr Khán	Governor of Iṣfáhán while the Báb was there. He was a Georgian by birth and an able governor. He accepted the message of the Báb and died soon after.
Mírzá Abu'l Qásim, Qá'im-Maqám-i-Faráhání	an able minister of the Qájárs. He was advisor to Crown Prince 'Abbás Mírzá and ensured that the eldest son of the late Crown Prince succeeded to the throne in 1834. In the first year of his reign, Muḥammad Sháh arranged for the murder of Qá'im-Maqám
Mírzá Asadu'lláh	a government official in Khuy near Chihríq. He became a Bábí and the Báb

	gave him the name ‘Dayyán’ which means ‘Judge’ or ‘Conqueror’
Mírzá Buzurg-i-Núrí	the father of Bahá’u’lláh. He was of a noble family of Mázindarán and held the post of Vizier to one of the Sháh’s sons
Mírzá Ḥasán Khán	a brother of the Grand Vizier who was ordered by him to carry out the execution of the Báb
Mírzá Ḥusayn-‘Alí	*see* Bahá’u’lláh
Mírzá Muḥammad-i-Khurásání	leader of the Shaykhí community in Ṭihrán and director of the school where Mullá Ḥusayn stayed in the city
Mirzá Muhít-i-Kirmání	a follower of Shaykh Aḥmad and Siyyid Káẓim who did not recognise the Báb but became a prominent Shaykhí leader
Mírzá Músá	a brother of Bahá’u’lláh who became His devoted follower
Mírzá Taqí Khán	Grand Vizier to Násiri’d-Dín Sháh. He was ousted from power and murdered in 1851
Mírzá Yaḥyá	a young half-brother of Bahá’u’lláh. He was appointed as official nominee of the Báb until such time as ‘He Whom God shall make manifest’ would appear and was given the title ‘Ṣubh-i-Azal’ (Morning of Eternity)
Muḥammad Big	a chief courier. He escorted the Báb from Iṣfáhán to Tabríz and became devoted to Him
Muḥammad Sháh	the third ruler of the Qájár dynasty (1834–48)
Mullá ‘Alíy-i-Basṭámí	a follower of Shaykh Aḥmad and Siyyid Káẓim who recognised the Báb, was named as a Letter of the Living and was

the first of the Báb's disciples to die for his faith

Mullá 'Alí-Akbar — a Bábí of Shíráz arrested along with Quddús and Mullá Ṣádiq

Mullá Ḥusayn-i-Bushrú'i — a student of Siyyid Káẓim, the first to search for the Promised One and the first to find Him. He was martyred in 1849 at Shaykh Ṭabarsí

Mullá Muḥammad — a student of Mírzá Muḥammad-i-Khurásání who helped Mullá Ḥusayn to deliver the Báb's letter to Bahá'u'lláh

Mullá Ṣádiq — an elderly religious leader of Shíráz who became a Bábí. He was cruelly beaten and driven from the city together with Quddús. His full name was Mullá Ṣádiq-i-Muqaddas-i-Khúrásání

Násiri'd-Dín Sháh — The fourth Qájár ruler (1848–96). He succeeded to the throne at seventeen and was assassinated in 1896

Prince Ḥamzih Mírzá — an army commander based near Mashhad who demanded Mullá Ḥusayn's presence at his camp

Quddús — Mullá Muḥammad-'Alíy-i-Barfurúshí, a student of Shaykh Aḥmad and Siyyid Káẓim who recognised the Báb. He was the youngest in years and the foremost in rank of the Letters of the Living. The title 'Quddús' (Holy) was given to him at the Conference of Badasht. He was martyred in Bárfurúsh in 1849

Sám Khán — colonel of the Armenian regiment given the task of shooting the Báb

Sayyáḥ — Mirzá 'Alíy-i-Sayyáḥ, a Bábí sent by the Báb to pray on His behalf at the site

	of the massacre of Shaykh Ṭabarsí
Shaykh 'Ábid	the teacher of the school which the Báb attended. He later became a Bábí
Shaykh Aḥmad-i-Aḥsá'í	a Persian religious teacher who first foretold the coming of the Báb
Shaykh Ḥasan-i-Zunúzí	a follower of Shaykh Aḥmad and Siyyid Káẓim. He first met the Báb in Karbilá, later became a Bábí, was the first Bábí pilgrim to reach Máh-Kú and relates the story of Anís, his young relative
Sir Henry Layard	a British diplomat who left a written account of a meeting with Ḥájí Mírzá Áqásí
Siyyid Ḥusayn and Siyyid Ḥasan-i-Yazdí	two Bábí brothers whom the Báb chose to accompany Him in Ádhirbáyján
Siyyid Káẓim-i-Rashtí	an outstanding disciple of Shaykh Aḥmad, whom Shaykh Aḥmad appointed as his successor
Sulaymán Khán	a prominent Bábí who arranged for the rescue of the remains of the bodies of the Báb and Anís
Ṭáhirih	the only woman amongst the Letters of the Living, the Báb's first disciples. She was martyred in 1852. Born in a notable family of clergy in Qazvín, she became famous for her learning and poetry. Siyyid Káẓim named her 'Qurratu'l-Ayn' (Solace of the Eyes). She was given the title 'Ṭáhirih' (The Pure One) at the Conference of Badasht
Vaḥíd	Siyyid Yaḥyáy-i-Dárábí, an outstanding religious teacher in whom Muḥammad Sháh had complete confidence. The

	Sháh sent him to interview the Báb in Shíráz. He became a Bábí and the Báb give him the name 'Vaḥíd' which means 'Peerless' or 'Unique'. Vaḥíd was martyred in Nayríz in June 1850
Yaḥyá Khán	the governor of Chihríq prison, a brother-in-law of the Sháh. He too became devoted to the Báb and disobeyed government orders

SOME PERSIAN AND ARABIC TERMS

Amír	a title of respect given to someone in authority; it can mean lord, prince, governor or commander
Ḥájí	a title which is given to any Muslim who has made the pilgrimage to Mecca
Ḥajj	pilgrimage to Mecca
Imám	the title given to the twelve Shí'ih successors of the Prophet Muḥammad. It is also given to some important Muslim religious leaders
Imám-Jum'ih	a title given to the most important religious leader in a town or city. He is the chief of all the mullás (religious leaders) in that place
Ka'bih	The holiest place in the Muslim world, the 'Black Stone' at Mecca
Kalántar	a title meaning 'mayor' or leading civic official in any town or city
Masjid	a mosque
Mullá	a title given to a Muslim religious leader. It can also mean a judge or theologian
Mujtahid	a doctor of Muslim law
Navváb	a title of honour meaning 'highness'
Naw-Rúz	the traditional Persian New Year, celebrated also by Bahá'ís
Qájár	a Persian dynasty of Turkish origin (1794–1925)

Shaykh	a title of respect given to an elder, a wise old man or a man in authority, a professor and a superior of a dervish order
Shaykhí	a follower of Shaykh Aḥmad and Siyyid Káẓim; those of the Shaykhís who did not recognise the Báb continued as a sect of Islám
Surih	a chapter of the Holy Qur'án
'Ulamá	learned clergyman
Vizier	a high executive officer of state, a minister or councillor

N.B. The English noun 'divine' is used interchangeably with 'clergy'.

A FEW DATES

1743	Birth of Shaykh Aḥmad
1780s	Shaykh Aḥmad begins his journeys
1815/16	Siyyid Káẓim meets Shaykh Aḥmad in Yazd
1817	Birth of Bahá'u'lláh in Ṭihrán
1819	Birth of the Báb in Shíráz
1826	Death of Shaykh Aḥmad at Medina
1843	Death of Siyyid Káẓim in Karbilá
1844	Mullá Ḥusayn begins his search
	23 May – the Báb declares His mission to Mullá Ḥusayn in Shíráz
	December – the Báb is on pilgrimage at Mecca and Medina
1845	July – the Báb is brought to Shíráz
1846	September – the Báb leaves Shíráz for Iṣfáhán
1847	July – the Báb reaches Máh-Kú
1848	April – the Báb leaves Máh-Kú
	July – the Báb is brought before the convocation at Tabríz
	July – the Conference at Badasht
	21 July – Mullá Ḥusayn raises the Black Standard
	4 September – death of Muḥammad Sháh
	October – Mullá Ḥusayn and his companions reach Shaykh Ṭabarsí and the siege begins
1849	January – death of Mullá Ḥusayn
	May – death of Quddús
1850	February – death of the Seven Martyrs of Ṭihrán
	May – siege of Zanján begins
	June – death of Vaḥíd
	9 July – martyrdom of the Báb